Foreword

I'm not sure I ever saw Carlton Palmer play football. I mean 'play football' in the flesh. His time as a professional footballer coincided with one of my occasional disenchanted disconnections from the game. This one, the Carlton Palmer-era one, was caused by living abroad, supporting Birmingham City during one of their especially bad times, and the 1980s, during which football spectators were treated as if they had come to sate some shabby addiction rather than simply to exchange cash for entertainment.

When, eventually, I did come across him in the flesh, it was in Dubai, where we both worked at the same school. Carlton took his duties very seriously. The first time I saw him he was standing in or near the school's entrance. He was greeting parents and children, smiling and wishing them 'Gud-morn-nin'.

Actually, I didn't know it was Carlton Palmer.

'That bloke on the door looks like Carlton Palmer,' I said to one of the staff when I arrived at the school.

'It is Carlton Palmer,' he said.

Although I had momentarily fallen out of love with football, I still knew who Carlton Palmer was. The miniaturised Easter Island face, the Naomi Campbell lips, and the body assembled from old deckchairs and a Meccano set; all these were unmistakable traits.

When I watched England games on television, I was always intrigued by his awkwardly lanky interventions and loping gallops. Other footballers obviously hated playing against him. They snapped and snarled at him, frustrated they couldn't go past or through or round him. At times, he seemed to be all over the field, as if a tribe of Carlton Palmers had been let loose. One expected to see him pop up almost everywhere and at any time. Though not in Dubai and not at a school, holding open doors for small children.

I spent a little time with him in Dubai, though not much. Carlton could clearly drink, whereas I could not. Carlton was clearly a social animal, whereas I was not. Carlton was clearly a night owl, whereas I was not. Neither did we seem to be interested in the same things. He once spent quite a long time explaining to me why I should buy one make of land cruiser rather than another. I probably glazed over and as a consequence almost certainly bought the wrong vehicle.

But even then I was aware there was no side to him, by which I mean that he was neither double-dealing nor false. Even his occasional untruths were expressed with a kind of bulldog integrity. It was also apparent that he took people at face value; no matter who you were or what you might have done or how you earned your money, Carlton would – if he liked you – give you time.

Cut to Shanghai a few years later where we were re-united at a different school in a different country. Carlton came to watch a play I'd written, after which he approached me and asked if I'd be interested in writing a book about him.

To Paul

It Is What It Is
The Carlton Palmer Story

Carlton Palmer with Steven Jacobi

Vertical Editions
www.verticaleditions.com

" Enjoy "
Best wishes
Carlton Palmer

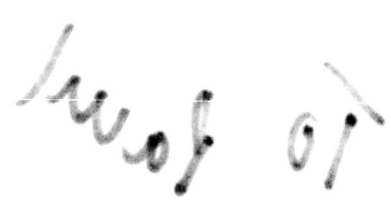

First published in the United Kingdom in 2017 by Vertical Editions, Unit 4a, Snaygill Industrial Estate, Skipton, North Yorkshire BD23 2QR

This edition published 2018

www.verticaleditions.com

ISBN 978-1-908847-11-9

A CIP catalogue record for this book is available from the British Library

Cover design by HBA, York

Printed and bound by Jellyfish Print Solutions, Swanmore, Hants

This book is dedicated to my family, without whose support, over all these years, I would not have achieved all I did. To my parents Lloyd and Linda, I thank you for all you have given me, not least your love and guidance. You showed me the way and I followed.

Thank you to my sisters Julie and Sharon, who have followed me around the country and also across the world to support me playing football. A special mention to my brother-in-law Phil, who in a time of need was there to help me. I will never forget yours and Sharon's kindness.

To my nieces Phoebe and Aoife, I love you lots (they will be so pleased).

To my children Kelly, Nicole and Jordan, you are my world and I'm so proud of you. I hope in reading this book you understand a little bit more about me and the unconditional love that I have for you.

To Amy my stepdaughter for nearly fifteen years, I love you dearly. I will always want the best for you. And no matter what, I will always be there for you when you need me.

Last but not least to my wife Lucy. You came into my life at a time when it seemed I had lost everything. You gave me love, you loved and cared for my children and you allowed me to be myself again – good or bad. I have only ever truly loved one woman and will only ever love one woman in the future and that is you.

Carlton Palmer

Contents

Acknowledgements

I would like to thank Dr. Steven Jacobi for taking a year out of his life to write my book. Steve, you know I aim to be successful in everything I do, but to me just writing the book was a success because it allowed me to reflect on my achievements, my disappointments and to apply closure to some aspects of my life which have long needed a lid putting on them. I carry a great deal of pride from my past into the future but I hope that by undertaking this process it helps me to become a better person too.

To Karl Waddicor at Vertical Editions, I thank you for agreeing to publish my book and for your hard work and support.

To my good friend Paul Muir, thank you for your help with the title and marketing of the book.

And to Kate Hamer, thank you for your help with publicising the book, setting up the launch events and bringing everything together. If this book is a success, it will be in no small part due to your contribution.

Carlton Palmer
www.carltonpalmer.com

'What kind of book?'

'My autobiography.'

A few years ago I'd collaborated in the writing of an actor's autobiography, so I knew the form and was, so long as the subject interested me, curious.

I asked Carlton to elaborate and he explained that he'd been thinking of writing a book for several years (had, indeed, received offers) but that he'd always held back. He wanted to write something that wasn't a conventional football book and that might crossover to another audience. Having watched my play, he thought he'd stumbled across an appropriate scribe, by which I assumed he meant a writer who didn't know much about football and wouldn't be obsessed by the usual things that football writers are supposed to be obsessed by.

So we arranged to meet, usually once a week, to talk and to try and piece together his story. Carlton didn't want the story to go from A-Z, so the story moves about a bit. Carlton didn't want the story to be all about football, so the story isn't all about football. Carlton wanted the story to be honest, so the story – up to a point, though some things are best left unsaid – is honest.

A few things struck me once we'd got to know one another. First, Carlton is no fool. He has a literal, dogged, untutored kind of intelligence, but it is still a piercing, disarmingly logical and alluring kind of intelligence. For this reason, I decided to write the book as if Carlton had been more conventionally educated – the way he talks here is the way he would probably talk if he'd had the schooling to fashion his thoughts.

Incidentally, he talks a little like he once played – with a confrontational, in-your-face style that nullifies vanity and pointless artifice; with epic bursts of energy, these occasionally interrupted by unexpected bursts of sophistication and grace.

Other things I learnt about him were his dedication (both to people and to keeping himself fit as a flea), his old-fashioned morality (mid-Victorian), his sense of humour (irony free though surprisingly wry), his curiously humble brand of vanity (sportswear chic), and his dislike of losing (at *anything*). I also discovered that we lived at different times in the same part of Birmingham. Initially, I wondered if this might afford a shared perspective on life, a bond of some sort, though I don't think that's right. He was a working class black boy who got spat out, whereas I was a middle-class white boy who (because of his father's financial frailties) got sucked back in.

The other thing I discovered was that the other book I really want to write about Carlton lies in the future. It is the one in which, after retirement, he learns to play golf. The kit and the etiquette and the game itself; Carlton's incongruous relationship with these would be comedy gold. The knitwear and slacks; the call for restrained and decorous behaviour; the physique that is all levers and projecting limbs attempting to swing with a degree of casual elegance something that looks in his hands like an unwanted toy.

One more thing that needs to be said. At the time of writing this, a month or so ago, Carlton's heart started to misbehave and he was rushed to hospital. So ill was he that the person accompanying him said that Carlton 'turned white'. Tests were inconclusive and two weeks ago he went to Singapore to play in a tournament to represent a team of England veterans. Carlton collapsed and was, once again, taken to hospital. This time, his heart stopped. Rubberised paddles were attached to his body. He was shocked back into life by electrical jolts. Next week, he will undergo a four-hour operation that will hopefully put right the problem. Carlton sent me a text from Singapore saying that he was literally scared for his life.

My immediate reaction was that his passing would be impossible to imagine. But fleetingly contemplating this, I was reminded of the question once put to the poet Philip Larkin: 'Do you feel you could have had a much happier life?'

'Not without being someone else,' Larkin replied.

If Carlton had been a snooker player – another game with comic possibilities – he would have been called Powerful Palmer, or Peppy Palmer, or Positive Palmer, or Perpetual Palmer, or Persistent Palmer. His life has a kinetic, infinitely inextinguishable quality. This book, then, is an attempt to capture bits of it in a relatively few short pages. The life is teeming, lively, bustling, occasionally infuriating, rarely dull. With luck, the writing reflects a little of this.

Steven Jacobi

1

The M69: The End of the Road

'It's a long old road, but I know I'm gonna find the end.'
Bessie Smith

The team bus, en route back to Coventry after the game at Highbury, dropped me at the service area on the M69. It was where I had left my car and from where I would drive back to Sheffield, where I lived. But I was a different man to the one who had parked up a few hours ago. Something had changed. Nothing physical. Although I was thirty-seven and in the twilight years of my career, my body still felt ok.

When he'd signed me, the manager at Coventry, Gordon Strachan, had offered me the choice of only coming into training two or three days a week. I suppose he was being sensitive about the journey I had to make down from Sheffield. Or sensitive about my age. But I didn't want to take the piss. Football was a job – a good job, the job I wanted to do, the only job I knew *how* to do – but still a job. I was lucky to have it and I was on good money, so I didn't want to take advantage. Strachan and I had played together at Leeds – he was a friend as well as a boss. Still. Never take the piss. That's what my dad had always told me.

Physically, I felt fine when I unlocked the car, took the wheel, and began driving back to Sheffield. Same as always. I didn't have to ease myself gingerly into the seat. I didn't have to swivel myself carefully into position. I didn't feel twinges in my back. My knees didn't lock. My cartilage wasn't scraping against bone.

All the same, something inside me had shifted.

Something fundamental had been emptied out of me and I felt momentarily unoccupied.

But I wasn't especially sad or unhappy. If anything, I was relieved.

Something long festering inside me now had a reason of expressing itself. An excuse and a pretext for saying out loud what had been bothering me for a quite a while. After sixteen years, I was through with being a footballer. Sixteen years in which I'd represented six clubs, made around five hundred appearances, collected eighteen England caps, and made in the region of five million quid.

But enough was enough.

My name is Carlton Palmer. I am fifty years old. Although I used to be a professional footballer I have not been a professional footballer for fourteen years. I currently live in Shanghai with my wife, Lucy. I coach football and run an academy at Wellington College. The apartment I live in is serviced, which means I don't even have to make our bed in the morning. Breakfast is provided. Someone does the washing and ironing. Clean towels are supplied on a daily basis. I go on nice holidays. Back in England, I own a large house. And when I get pissed off with the weather, I go to my other house in Portugal. All this – the job and the lifestyle – is a legacy of being able to kick a football and run like fuck around a relatively small area of over-manicured grass. It's a strange thing to have done and a curious way to have made a living. I loved it while it was happening and then, when the time came, I knew that I had fallen out of love with the game. One sunny afternoon in London, in front of thirty-eight thousand people, football and I looked at each other and decided to call it a day.

I had always liked playing at Highbury. The pitch, unwrinkled and silky, like baize, like the kind of carpet we'd never been able to afford in the house in which I was raised. The marble halls, the sense of history, knowing that in playing Arsenal you were playing one of the best teams in the country.

It was the sort of game you looked forward to as a player. The sort of game that legitimised you as a professional footballer. The sort of game that challenged you.

It was a hot day. Arsenal were a year or so away from becoming 'The Invincibles', the team that won the championship while remaining unbeaten throughout an entire season. But the players that formed the nucleus of that side were already in place. I knew they were good players and had played against many of them for a number of years.

I can't recall the exact date but I can remember standing in the tunnel, anticipating the battle, relishing it. I knew some of them from playing for England – Adams, Seaman, Dixon, Parlour, Keown – and others I had come to admire as great players … Bergkamp, Vieira and Pires, for example.

I always liked to be the last one onto the pitch, which meant I was usually at the end of the line of players nervously shuffling and fidgeting, waiting for the signal to head out into the Highbury sunshine. Vieira looked at me, wished me well, and touched me lightly on the shoulder as he loped past me to take up his own position.

We'd had some good clashes over the years. Same kind of player. Long legs, good engine, an appetite for work. We spent much of the game in each other's eyeline, tracking backwards and forwards, trying to stop the other from dictating play.

Bryan Robson once said to me before we went onto the field at Old Trafford, 'Don't try to keep up with me, Carlton. I'll run you into the fucking ground. I'll take you all over this fucking pitch, to every corner. I'll run the fucking legs off you.'

Same deal with Vieira. Except he was big. All the Arsenal team were big. Especially Petit. Bergkamp, too. Even *Dixon*. But Vieira was biggest of all.

His style suited me. He was always looking for the ball, which meant he was constantly going into areas where I could control him. Having the same body shape meant that I instinctively understood where his physique might take him and at what kinds of speed. I also knew that nobody could 'run' me over forty or fifty yards. We were both all arms and legs, and looked as though we'd been stapled together from bits of old deckchairs.

So I liked playing against Vieira. It's like boxing: fights are made by styles. And he suited my style.

That day was the second time I had come up against Thierry Henry. He'd been signed from Juventus for eleven million quid at the beginning of the season and although he'd shown signs of brilliance, the talk around clubs was that he was inconsistent and with the right kind of attention could be kept quiet. In December, we'd beaten the Gunners 3-2 at Highfield Road. It was probably our best performance of the season and we were confident that we could get something at Highbury.

Before the game, Strachan was worried about Henry. 'Stay close to him, Carlton,' he told me. 'Don't give him too much space to run into.'

This made sense. Because of injuries, I was playing a more defensive role than usual. I wouldn't be so much scrapping with Vieira as shielding the defence, sometimes even becoming a defender.

I watched Henry warming up and saw a lithe greyhound of a man, nimble and alert, but nothing that I couldn't handle. I was used to playing against people who were quicker than me, or thought they were quicker than me, and reckoned that if their pace wasn't enough, then their skill would be enough to create time and space for them to do damage. What they never bargained for was that I could read the game and that my levers – my arms and legs – often allowed me to get in a leg or another part of my body at the moment when a player thought he'd got away from me.

The first forty-five minutes went more or less according to plan. We hadn't won away from home the whole season but we weren't a bad side and had some good defenders. Arsenal had been playing in Europe that week, so maybe that had an effect on their performance. All the same, they didn't seem to be especially sluggish and we went in, pleased with ourselves, at 0-0. Strachan was satisfied and reminded me to keep tight on Henry. Maybe he saw something that I'd missed as he prompted me more than once. Sure, Henry had got away from me once or twice but on the whole I felt things were under control.

Then it all started to go wrong.

About five minutes into the second half, Vieira passed

to Henry, who had a thirty or forty yard run-in on goal. We were playing quite a high line and I was caught marginally out of position – not close enough to Vieira to prevent the pass, not tight enough on Henry to close him down. All the same, I backed myself to catch him. But for the first time in my career, I found myself not able to make-up the ground. Worse, Henry was jetting away from me with nonchalant ease, his legs moving him towards the penalty area with oiled, supple elegance. My legs were working fine, or at least as they usually did, like a couple of methodical pistons, and doing their normal, efficient job. But it wasn't enough. Nowhere near enough. Henry was completely indifferent to me because he knew that I would never catch him. I don't think he even bothered to look over his shoulder to check where I might be.

As Steve Ogrizovic came out to narrow the angle, Henry side-footed it past him into the net. His seventeenth goal of the season. 1-0 to the Arsenal.

Gary McAllister must have noticed something about the alarmed expression on my face.

'You all right, Carlton?' he said.

'Yeah. No worries,' I replied.

I experienced the rest of the game in a kind of slow-motion blur. Every time I tried to deny him space, he moved into a wide position. Every time I made an effort to push him into areas where I could contain him, he managed to find new ones to exploit. Short of chaining him to me or pegging him to the ground, I tried everything to stop him getting away. When I tried tackling him on his first touch, Vieira and Bergkamp simply played the ball in behind me. If I gave Henry room, he merely glided past me. I ended up spending forty minutes permanently out of position just because there was no position I could take that would enable me to prevent Henry doing what the fuck he wanted. He had pace, movement, control, power, and skill; the best player I've ever come across. I couldn't catch him. I couldn't stop him. I couldn't get near him. I was a lumbering fool to Henry's will-o'-the-wisp. It wasn't pleasant and I ended the game knackered, having achieved only one thing: the realisation that I had to stop playing football for a living.

At the end of the game, I remember feeling not dismay or horror – things had gone way beyond that – but relief. Like a weight had been lifted from my shoulders. Carlton, I thought, you've had a good run for your money. Stop now. It was so simple and I was almost at ease with myself.

We lost 3-0 and in the dressing room afterwards, Strachan came over to me.

'I think that's it for me,' I said.

'What do you mean?'

'I mean, that's it. No more.'

'You're not serious.'

'I fucking am serious. I'm finished. I'm retiring.'

He tried to talk me out of it and I knew, for all kinds of reasons, that I couldn't really just stop playing then and there. Strachan had invested time and money in me. I also had a contract, of course. And I owed him something; he was undoubtedly a good football man. He'd also tried to treat me with understanding. He knew I liked a drink, for example, and didn't require me to come in for training on Mondays. 'I don't want you smelling of booze and setting a bad example,' was how he expressed it, but there was also sensitivity behind what he said. All the same, inside *I knew*. A decision had been made.

Of course, life is never as simple as you'd like it to be.

Although I knew that as a top-class player I was finished – and I didn't want to drop down the divisions, stop being a top-class player, and just be *a player* – I was still a Coventry player at the end of the season and was still trying to get fit on the club's pre-season training programme at St Andrew's, Scotland, in July.

How the fuck had that happened?

For one thing, I'd spoken about my retirement plans to Ron Atkinson, a manager I'd known since I was a teenager. It was the first thing I'd done after the Arsenal game. The team coach had dropped me at the M69 service area and I'd driven home to Sheffield.

'Don't be a fool, Carlton,' Ron said when I told him of my decision.

'I've made up my mind, Ron.'

'Because of one bad game?'

'It wasn't just a bad game.'

'Thierry-fucking-Henry can do that to anyone. He's lightning. The best there is. Don't worry about it.'

'I'm not.'

'If you stop playing, you'll regret it.'

'I will stop playing and I won't regret it.'

'How do you know you won't regret it? Everyone who stops playing regrets it.'

'I won't regret it and I won't miss it.'

'Think about it.'

'I don't need to think about it.'

'You don't need to think about it?'

'No.'

'Of course you need to think about it. It's the thing you need to think about more than anything else.'

'No. It's obvious to me. I've had a feeling about it for

a long time. The Arsenal game just made me understand what that feeling meant.'

'You'll still regret it.'

'For fuck's sake, Ron. It's actually a relief.'

'What does that mean?'

'It is what it is. I'm through. Maybe not right now but pretty soon. As soon as I can.'

All the same, I had always listened to Ron and it's possible that despite knowing in my bones that I was finished, his words calmed me down, made me hesitate.

There was another reason, however.

Driving back to Sheffield, I was also plotting the end of my marriage. Jenny and I had been together for the most part of my professional career. At that point in time, we had three children, lived in a large house, went on great holidays, and had everything we could reasonably want. But, as with my football, I felt that something long sickening within me needed to be put out of its misery.

I wanted a divorce.

Things between Jenny and I had not been good for a while. Years, in fact. We had grown apart and become two different people. Even Jenny knew it. 'We've done our time,' she said, on one of the few occasions we actually talked about ending the marriage. Nineteen years of time, in fact, making it sound like a prison sentence, which was something it was gradually coming to resemble. She wanted to move back to Birmingham. She was tired of living in a big house and always living in the spotlight. She wanted to be closer to her friends. The house had sixty-four radiators. I know because one mad morning I counted them. To be frank, I'm not sure what Jenny wanted but I also felt the need for something different. I had a girlfriend but she was nothing to do with the strong feeling that as well as ending my playing career I should also end my marriage to Jenny.

So, driving back to Sheffield I was making firm plans for a new life. An existence that didn't include playing football or a wife. A clean break. A new direction. A fresh start. My expectations of life were changing – had changed – and I was going to embrace them.

In the car by myself it all seemed so straightforward and clear. I made some calculations about my net worth. Could I afford to lose my livelihood and my marriage at the same time? The house was worth £1.1 million. I had two houses in Portugal valued at, say, £600,000. I had a pension: £5 million. I was still earning and had another two years at Coventry if I wanted them, which was reassuring even if I didn't want them. But the solicitor said it would cost me at least £2 million to divorce Jenny. Probably more. So maybe I would need to keep playing in order to finance the divorce? Or perhaps it would be better to stop playing and hang onto the marriage for a bit longer? Or possibly I should just do what I felt was the right thing and walk away from the playing and the marriage at the same time, and fuck the consequences?

A few days later, and I had neither called time on my career nor my marriage.

The clarity I thought I had achieved was obscured by indecision, practicality and inertia. I thought about the kids. I thought about my mum and dad. I thought about honouring my contract at Coventry. I thought about the people I would be letting down. I thought about everything except what was gnawing away inside me.

And that's why I ended up doing pre-season in St. Andrew's.

At one point, having been forbidden to go out by Strachan, who was worried about our conspicuousness in the sleepy university town, John Hartson and I hired a stretch limo and drove to the Old Course Hotel. We booked a suite and I, at least, had every intention of misbehaving discreetly. Then Hartson went missing and I found him on a stage in the bar, singing, clearly pissed. (He could afford to; he'd already negotiated a move to Celtic, something he'd forgotten to tell me.) Strachan was furious and our relationship took a turn for the worse. He left me out of the team at the beginning of the season. Immediately, I wanted 'out' and began to regret not being stronger about the decision I'd made after the Arsenal game four months ago. Then it all got a bit messy. Watford wanted me on loan, which I agreed to, only to be recalled after five matches, play a couple of games for Coventry, then go back to my former club Sheffield Wednesday on loan. Initially, I was reluctant to go because of the good times I'd had there earlier in my career, but Ron Atkinson asked me as a favour. Peter Shreeves was the manager and Wednesday were in trouble, battling relegation. I was offered £5,000 per game on top of my salary and a bonus of £60,000 if we stayed up. In other words, it was worth my while to go back and I would be putting money in the bank for the day when I stopped playing and I stopped being married to Jenny.

The clarity of the decision I'd made driving back to Sheffield that night had been compromised by expediency and convenience. There was just about enough for me financially and professionally to justify playing on despite the persistent, nagging feeling that I was a dead man walking. I even felt that because I loved the club, helping Wednesday to stay up was somehow not only a noble thing to do but was in some way written in the stars.

All bollocks, of course.

As a professional footballer, you're encouraged to believe that you are in control of your destiny. That your life and career can be manipulated and controlled. That everything has some kind of purpose. Football was all I ever wanted to do and all I had done. Even the decision to stop doing it had been made with the same sense of certainty and confidence. So how did I explain to myself that I was still playing and I was still married? I must have decided that these were the best courses of action to take, mustn't I? But what I'd liked or wanted to think and what is actually true are not the same. I know that now. So this, in part, is the story of Carlton Palmer, an ex-footballer who for sixteen years did a job he loved and was paid very well for it. Who for many of those sixteen years stayed in the best hotels and ate the best food and drank the best drinks and wore the best clothes and drove the best cars and had relationships with the best-looking women and was looked after by the best doctors. Who came to realise that life wasn't as straightforward as it once seemed. Who has conveniently forgotten about the boredom and the physical pain and the silliness of it all but who, every Saturday, even though he hasn't pulled on a pair of football boots in anger for thirteen years or so, is not ashamed to say that he still gets an excited tingle of anticipation.

2

Rowley Regis: The Comforts of Home

'Charity begins at home, and justice begins next door.'
Charles Dickens

It's conventional to start a story like this with stuff about your childhood. Mine happened in Rowley Regis, which is somewhere in the West Midlands. We moved there when I was ten or eleven from Oldbury, where I was born. But like all places these days, the original village has grown and developed and merged with other places to become part of a conurbation. That was the kind of word I remember being used by my Geography teacher at St Michael's Church of England School, which wasn't – to my dad's kindly irritation – the grammar school, where he doubtless would have wanted me to go. Other people went there, like the comedian Josie Lawrence and the bloke that played bass for Dexys Midnight Runners. But not me.

On the other hand, I wasn't a rebel or anything like that. I suppose it might be more dramatic if I was able to tell a story of poverty, hardship, racial abuse, ghettoised resentment, brushes with the law, and so on and so forth.

You know, with me using football as a means of escaping from a life of drug addiction and crime. That sort of thing. But it wasn't like that. Not in the slightest.

While I was growing up, I spent my time not getting into trouble, not doing drugs, and not feeling like some kind of disenfranchised outsider. I spent my time not getting girlfriends up the duff (in fact, not getting girlfriends *at all*), not getting drunk, not doing badly at school, not being particularly unhappy, and not hanging aimlessly around the park. I spent my time not getting into fights, not making many friends, and not being kicked out of school.

So what did I spend my time doing?

I spent my time playing and watching football. From a relatively early age, that's what I did and what I wanted to do. When the school got in some fart to give us careers advice, he pointed me in the direction of becoming a postal worker or some such shit. 'A postal worker?' I remember thinking. 'A fucking postal worker?!' How should any fourteen-year old boy react to this information, the news that he is destined to spend the rest of his life as a postal worker, whatever that is. When I told him I wanted to be a professional footballer, he didn't so much laugh as just ignore what I'd said. 'Yeah, yeah, son,' his blank, incurious expression seemed to be saying, 'we've heard it all before. And no doubt you'll want to play for England, too. Ha ha.'

Years later, after I'd become a professional footballer and played for England, I turned up for a school reunion at St Michael's. I arrived in a stretch limo, wearing a Versace suit, looking expensive. I probably strutted around a lot being insufferable and exuding a 'fuck off, cunts' attitude … you know, 'Postal worker, eh?! Shove *that* up your arse.' Having become successful, the comedian Bob Monkhouse once observed, 'They laughed at me when I said I wanted to be a comedian. Well, they're not laughing now.' I suppose I felt the same way even though, in point of fact, I was acting like a wanker. All the same, I reckoned I'd earned the right to act like one.

I was always trying to prove people wrong. I was cussed and annoyingly stubborn. Maybe I'd have become a postal worker if the careers guy had told me, 'Listen, Carlton. I reckon you ought to become a professional footballer. I think becoming a postal worker is beyond your reach. Sorry, son. That's just the way it is.'

This obduracy and pig-headedness, a kind of iron-willed determination, came from my father. Lloyd George Palmer arrived from Jamaica in the late 1950s, drove Midland Red buses, and set about building a good life for the family he was creating. I was the middle one of three – the other two were girls – and maybe this feeling of being sandwiched between two unfamiliar women has something to do with my instinctive urge to prove people wrong, make myself heard, and to fight a corner.

But really, I think, it's mostly about my dad who, I now understand, I am very like. We even look the same. He was – is – a hard man. He boxed in the army, was completely uncompromising, and absolutely determined to improve himself. He was an intelligent man who read books and had impeccable manners while at the same time being principled and argumentative. He could be kind and generous when he needed to be but his warm heart was nearly always tempered by logic and pragmatism. He always needed to see the reason for something, not least the way he behaved towards his children.

Although we didn't have much money, we were never

poor and dad always made sure we had good Christmas presents. I once worked out that the presents he'd bought for us, his three kids, would have set him back the equivalent of two weeks' wages. When I signed professional forms for West Bromwich Albion, I was almost immediately earning more than him. If he begrudged this or felt aggrieved, he never showed it. Neither did he ask me for anything, least of all money. I once gave him a car though I had to pretend that the car was not actually from me but surplus to club requirements – otherwise, he would not have accepted it. It was dad who insisted that I buy a house when I became a professional footballer. This was the last thing I wanted to do – what kind of teenager wants to buy a fucking house?! – But it was the best advice anyone has ever given me. I bought a small terraced house for £21,000 and sold it on a few years later for £36,000. Dad did the work on it, decorating and repairing, knowing and understanding that I would never get round to it.

Although he wasn't a physical man, or not conspicuously so, he wasn't afraid of *being* physical. A few times he took the slipper to me when I got bad grades or was in danger of falling behind with my studies. He was determined that we should all do well and be successful, which for him meant going to university. My two sisters did go on to college and get their degrees but I was never likely to go … not if I had my way about becoming a footballer. Although we never talked about, or didn't talk about it explicitly, dad paid me the compliment of never advising me against it. But he still wanted me to do well enough at school to go to university, just in case. I can still remember his speech on my wedding day, which included the line, 'If I'd known Carlton would be so successful, I would have been kinder to him'.

Actually, he *was* kind to me, but kind in the best way possible. He bequeathed me values, determination and desire. Ever since, I've responded well to a series of father figures, not because I didn't have a father but because I had a bloody good one and I wanted more of the same. There was a P.E. teacher at school who always gave me good advice and encouraged me. Harry Maney was the first real father figure, though. He was the manager of my Sunday team, Newton Albion. Roy Horobin, a scout for West Bromwich Albion, was another. And Ron Atkinson, of course.

The thing that all three had in common was that they kept me earthed and stopped me becoming too much of a wanker whenever becoming too much of a wanker loomed as a real possibility. Soon after I'd established myself as a first team player at Albion, I walked into Big Ron's office and asked him whether I still needed to do the chores I'd been assigned as a youth team player, things like cleaning boots and scrubbing down the changing rooms. Ron didn't even look up from his desk. 'Do me a favour, CP,' he said, 'fuck off and make sure you close the door on the way out.'

World Cup winner Nobby Stiles, the youth team coach at Albion, was another influence. In his days as a player, he was known as a brilliant man marker though I didn't realise until I worked with him how good he was. For some reason, we hit it off and he took a real interest in me. As a small man, he knew what he had to do to compete at the highest level, which was basically to read the game and never to switch off or stop thinking about your job. But he also worked on the physical side of my game, spending hours walking me through match situations, using old car tyres as a way of teaching me to shorten my stride, making sure I learnt how to stay low and jockey other players, and always being alert so that I was in the right position.

I listened to people like Roy and Harry and Nobby and Ron not just because they were good at what they did but because in some ways they reminded me of my dad. Plus all of them were determined, resolute and uncompromising. I saw this in the way dad presented himself in company – proud, unbending, bloody-minded. Smartly dressed, always punctual, unfailingly courteous. I used to love watching him play snooker at the local club. He would never admit how much he hated to lose but you could see the competitiveness and the steel pulsing just beneath the civil, respectful surface. Generous and kind when he needed to be, but if you ever crossed him or pissed him off, he would cut you out of his life … brutally and forever. He was the original 'fit in or fuck off' merchant.

These are traits I recognise in myself and, for better or worse, I have tried to bring up my own kids more or less in the same way. The big difference between us is that while he was always calm and calculated, I have a tendency to boil over. I boiled over only last week, in a McDonald's restaurant in Shanghai. I overheard three white guys abusing an Arab who happened to be in the restaurant. This was immediately after the Isis attacks on Paris, so there was a context, though no circumstances could excuse the vicious verbal assault that was taking place. The insults and the foul language weren't directed at me and in any case I'd received my fair share of taunting over the years and learnt to be immune. But for some reason those three ignorant prats got under my skin. At any rate, I saw red and told them to shut up and fuck off, or they'd have to answer to me. There was an exchange of views and, before I knew it, I had one of them by the neck, marched him outside, and pinned him against a wall. Though that was, more or less, where it ended

Afterwards, I thought how dad would have handled it. 'Differently' was all I could think of. I doubt there would have been a scene though if he'd been offended and wanted to make a point, he would have moved from quiet, passive irritation to stern patriarch in a trice. No unseemly neck holding from him; just an explosive blur of anger.

Dad was actually very businesslike about racial prejudice. 'It exists,' was all he said about it to me, 'so just accept it.' Some people have accused me of being flippant and indifferent about racism but my dad taught me that racial abuse was never an excuse to behave badly. 'If you're the best, race doesn't exist' was another of the things he used to say to me. I know this won't play well with liberal thinkers who believe that racism is intolerable in any situation, regardless of how good or bad the person being abused might be, but dad was merely trying to be realistic, make sure I learnt to stand up for myself, and didn't become a moaner.

So when I grabbed that small-minded bigot of a fucker by the throat in McDonald's, my immediate thought was that I had in some way let down my dad. He was a proud Jamaican but also proud to be British. He would have failed Norman Tebbit's 1990 cricket test and failed it with pride. His heart was generous enough and his mind sophisticated enough to accommodate two cultures and two countries, loving both with equal intensity.

He readily and quickly embraced the traditions of his new country, one of which was watching *Match of the Day* on Saturday night. So it is perhaps appropriate that when he had a heart attack a few years ago, it was while he was watching the programme. Mum had already gone to bed and rather than wake her up, he crawled to the kitchen and somehow downed a couple of aspirin. These thinned his blood and probably prevented him having a stroke. When mum found him in the morning, curled up on the floor, she called an ambulance. He should have been dead. The ambulance crew and the doctors couldn't believe he'd survived the attack. But that was dad all over: unfussy, strong, contrary. A right awkward bugger, in fact. Growing up, I was always closer to my mum but I have *become* my dad. Still, if I was going to become a professional footballer, this was a lot better than being close to my dad but being my mum.

3

Black

'... he is what is known in some schools as a fucking lazy, thick nigger.' Ron Atkinson

Yesterday I was fifty. I celebrated the occasion in Shanghai, where I am now living. Lucy had arranged lunch at a bar called Liquid Laundry. We reserved two tables and friends dropped by during the afternoon, drinking and eating and chatting. I started with a bottle of white wine. Then champagne. By late afternoon, and after decamping to another bar over the road called Jenny's, I was knocking back the Guinness. Lucy stayed in Liquid Laundry with the girls while us blokes got lathered. When she found me later, I had fallen asleep. Drunk, of course. She wrestled me into a taxi and then somehow got me to the apartment and, eventually, into bed, where I slept until midnight.

When I woke up, I felt hungry. Lucy was asleep beside me.

'I'm hungry,' I said.

No reply.

'I need food.'

Still no reply.

'I need food.'

'What?'

'I'm hungry.'

'Don't wake me up, Carlton.'

'So you want anything to eat?'

'No.'

'Fancy a McDonald's?'

'What?'

'Fancy a McDonald's?'

'No. I do not fancy a McDonald's.'

'Oh.'

'Oh *what*?'

'I'm hungry.'

'For fuck's sake, Carlton. Go and find something in the fridge.'

'Are you angry?'

'You've woken me up.'

'Have I?'

'Yes.'

'Sorry.'

'Bit late now.'

'Sorry.'

I suppose it was a bit late. And, as Lucy always points out, I always drink on an empty stomach, so not only do I feel hungry later, but I also get inebriated pretty fast. In the morning, I would get up at about 6 a.m. and go to the gym for ninety minutes and sweat out all the alcohol. That's what I've always done and even though I don't particularly like going to the gym, I guess it's become a deep-rooted habit, entrenched from my playing days. Lucy says I should just drink less and then I wouldn't have to put myself through the pain barrier on such a regular basis. But that wouldn't work. Not for me, at least. I like drink. I like drinking. I like being drunk.

I stumbled to the kitchen and opened the fridge door. My mind was still scrambled and I couldn't remember much of what happened after we arrived at Liquid Laundry. Trying to put my mind in order, I recall eating a light breakfast (two eggs and toast) and then going shopping on the Huaihai Road. It's a bit weird being in China at Christmas. All the shops are geared up for it – Christmas trees, decorations, the lot – but for all the show, the Chinese don't really celebrate Christmas. Most only have a day off work. It's just an opportunity to sell stuff.

Anyway, I'd be going home to Sheffield in a week and spending Christmas in England. I was looking forward to it. Christmas and summer are the best times to be in England. When I got back, I'd see my kids, watch some football, do some television punditry (which would pay for the trip), and generally catch up with people, including my mum and dad. Much as I like Shanghai, I was looking forward to it.

So that was in my mind as looked at the contents of the fridge.

Another thing I remembered from the morning was walking through a mall and seeing some kind of display that was advertising the new *Star Wars* film *The Force Awakens*. It filled more or less the whole of the lobby. There was a replica Starfighter and a small platoon of life-sized Stormtroopers. A couple of thin, very pale-skinned Caucasian women perched on high heels were standing in front of the Starfighter offering to have their photograph taken with anyone who wanted it. There were plenty of volunteers even though one of the girls had a face like a parrot.

There was also a poster for the film. There was something odd about it and for a moment I couldn't work out what it was. Then it clicked. The Chinese poster was different from other posters I'd seen on the internet. The British actor, John Boyega, who features prominently on all other notices, as he should do because he's a prominent character in the film, had been relegated to the supporting cast. The size of his image had been minimalised.

John Boyega, by the way, is a black actor.

It was the same when *12 Years a Slave* came out in 2013 and the poster implied that its star, the black actor Chiwetel Ejiofor, was a relatively minor character in the drama.

Both of these instances are examples of attempts to make the films more appealing to Chinese audiences by downplaying the role of their black actors. The message is clear: Chinese people would not necessarily go to watch films which boasted black men and women as their stars.

As a rule, the Chinese don't like black people. Although I have rarely been treated badly here or felt discriminated against, I am periodically aware of people staring at me and I know that generally in China black people are perceived as being inferior. Fuck knows where this comes from though it's probably something to do with skin colour (dark skin is still associated with peasants and outdoor, manual labour) and vague ideas about black people derived from films and the media. Many Chinese people think that black people are violent and/or play basketball. There is also an assumption that black people do not have money, which for the Chinese, these days, is probably the main stigma.

Recently, I went to Singapore to play in a veterans game, Old England versus Old Germany. Whilst there, I bought Lucy a Rolex watch. When I returned to Shanghai, the officials stopped three people – me and two other men. We had one thing in common. We were all black. On finding Lucy's gift-wrapped watch (not that I was hiding it), they confiscated it, saying it would be returned when I left the country. Then there was a bit of trouble as I stood my ground and became defiant. They would have arrested me for swearing had not a Chinese woman explained to them that I had not sworn. I had the distinct impression that the police had targeted me because of my skin colour and were determined to find something they could use against me. In the end, taking the Rolex was enough. As I write, they still have it.

Generally speaking, however, I am isolated from this kind of racism. My job and my money keep me from coming into contact with it. But I know it exists, like a whisper – not quite able to be heard, but still able to be detected. Maybe the reason I took on the guy in McDonalds who was making racist comments about Muslims was a symptom of this awareness? Maybe I'd been bottling up my feelings about it? Maybe I was just using it as an excuse to be angry? Who knows?

Anyway, thinking about all this as I searched the fridge, my mind still a little scrambled and in free flow mode, looking for something to eat – ham for a sandwich or maybe some cheese, which costs an arm and a leg out here, and which I could eat with biscuits … even a fucking apple would do – I had a Proustian moment, my madeleine moment, and began to recall with sudden clarity the racism I'd experienced during my time in football.

Although I was more or less the only black kid at school in Rowley Regis (and sometimes it felt like we were the only black family in Rowley Regis), I don't recall anyone ever subjecting me to racial abuse. It would make a nice story – the black boy who was vilified at school using the pain and humiliation he experienced to turn himself into an international footballer as a means of proving himself, of getting his own back – but it didn't work like that. I rather liked school. And even when someone called me a 'black bastard' on the football field, it never *felt* like racism. The first time it happened, when I was playing for Newton Albion, it probably surprised and annoyed me, more because it was the first time than because of any hurt. Like your first mosquito bite. But after that, and partly because of the values my dad had instilled in me, I didn't take any notice when other players called me a 'black bastard'. They were only doing it to get a reaction, to put me off my game, and I never let it get to me. Anyway, I was called a 'black bastard' when I played for Newton Albion. I was called a 'black bastard' when I was having trials at Chelsea and Queen's Park Rangers. I was called a 'black bastard' when I played for West Bromwich Albion. I was called a 'black bastard' when I played for Sheffield Wednesday. I was called a 'black bastard' when I played for Leeds United. I was called a 'black bastard' when I played for Southampton. I was called a 'black bastard' when I played for Nottingham Forest. I was called a 'black bastard' when I played for Coventry City. I was called a 'black bastard' when I played for Watford. I was called a 'black bastard' when I played for Stockport County. I was called a 'black bastard when I played for Dublin City'. I was called a 'black bastard' when I played for Mansfield Town. Fucking hell, I was even called a 'black bastard' when I played for Staveley Miners Welfare. I have been called a 'black bastard' by individuals in crowds, by whole groups of supporters (*'You black bas-*

tard!'), by opposing managers, by opposing coaches, by ball boys, by kit men, by club mascots, and by the fat blokes who open the doors to the lounge areas at grounds. I have been called a 'black bastard' by a player who at the time was actually playing for the same team as me. I have been called a 'black bastard' by other black bastards, including Ian Wright, who I love to bits and is probably the biggest black bastard of them all. But despite being called a 'black bastard' by so many people, in so many places, and at so many times, it never once felt like racial abuse.

And I always gave as good as I got. For example, when I saw a ginger cunt I called him a 'ginger cunt' (Paul Scholes), but I don't think I have a narrow-minded prejudice against people with ginger hair. The thing is, when you play at the top level of any sport, you will do anything to gain an advantage. That's all it is. Trying to get the upper hand.

Most players understand this most of the time, though occasionally it does spill over. Once, in a derby match against Sheffield United, things got a bit tasty. United were a physical and lippy team, made in the image of their manager at that time, Neil Warnock. Ron Atkinson told me to 'keep a lid on it', knowing that I also liked to dish it out and fight fire with fire. Anyway, it started going off in the tunnel, before the game had even got under way. Somehow, the 'black bastard' taunts were more vicious and personal than was usual – it's difficult to explain, but you always *know* what people mean and how personal it is. Fortunately Danny Wilson could see the warning signs and sorted things out before the situation got out of hand.

Another time, Wednesday were playing Liverpool and I thought it would be good idea to get under Jan Molby's skin by calling him 'fat'. 'Why are you so fucking fat?' I started. 'Call yourself a fucking footballer?' Molby didn't even blink. He just turned to me and very quietly listed all the medals he'd won, the international caps he'd collected, and the material evidence of his successful career. He ended by offering me the keys to one of his holiday homes, which I was welcome to use once his team had beaten us. (Which they did, and Molby played a blinder.) 'Now fuck off,' he concluded.

In 1992, Wednesday played Hartlepool United in the cup. Hartlepool had a player called Brian Honour who started to try and wind me up in the tunnel before the game. It was the usual stuff and for some reason I gave it back with a bit extra, probably spending too much time asking him about his non-existent England caps, the piss-poor facilities at his club, the meagre win bonus he was on, the number of houses he owned, and so on and so forth. In other words, the usual crap. The next day, it was all over the newspapers. Honour accused me of being a big-time Charlie and said I'd spent the whole game belittling him and his club. Apparently, so I later learnt, the 'story' had come from his chairman. Even so, and even if I pushed things further than usual, it was just banter designed to undermine an opponent. So long as the abuse can be identified as part of the competitive cut and thrust, I don't take offence when insulting words are directed towards me.

I think what I am saying is that I do not feel that racism is especially prevalent in English football – if by 'racism' you mean actual prejudice and bigotry. Sure, racist language is used but racist language does not, in my book, necessarily constitute actual racism. There's a big difference between word and deed, especially in elite sports.

It follows that I don't have much time for people who

play the race card and either use it as an excuse for putting in a poor performance or hide behind it. When Mario Balotelli threatened to walk off the pitch the next time he was subjected to racist taunts, I was asked by Radio 5 Live for my opinion and how I would have dealt with the situation. I got into a bit of hot water when I responded by saying that his ultimatum showed weakness and that in all circumstances he should stay on the field and prove people wrong. 'That's what I would have done,' was the gist of it. I think I even said that if someone threw a banana at me, I hoped I would have the wit simply to pick it up and eat it.

Subsequently, Stan Collymore, John Barnes and Ian Wright contacted me to take issue with what I'd said, suggesting I was being frivolous about racism, that it was an important issue, and I was not taking the matter seriously enough.

In point of fact, I was asked by the BBC for a reaction without knowing the full facts behind Balotelli's threat to walk off the field. Nor had I managed to find out its full context as I'd been on a flight from Dubai when the news broke. Afterwards, I even wondered whether I'd been stitched-up because the BBC knew I'd give a straight answer. Nevertheless, my point still stands: whilst racism has no place in football, people should not confuse racist comments with the intent of racial hatred. And unless there is clear evidence that actual racism is part of the perpetrator's purpose, neither should players or anyone else dwell on it. If someone tries to wind me up by referring to the colour of my skin, I think it's because I'm playing well enough to be perceived as a threat. In a way, it's a kind of compliment. And always at the back of my mind is the thought that if I reacted to mere words then I would be letting down my mum and dad.

Still, I understand that racist flashpoints sell newspapers, even if it constitutes a lazy form of journalism. If pushed, I would say that racism is more subtly embedded in the game. You never hear, for example, of chairmen or managers threatening to take their players off the field for racial abuse. They've got too much to lose. The wrong people, i.e. the players, always end up getting stick for these things whereas the matter is less obviously but more deeply rooted off the field.

Here's an example. When I stopped playing I did some punditry for the BBC, starting at more or less the same time as people like Lee Dixon, Martin Keown and Alan Shearer. I did *Football Focus* and a few editions of *Match of the Day*. I took it all very seriously and went to media lessons, which focused on things like teaching me not to repeat words and pretending that I was speaking to non-experts. I boned up on statistics, had a working knowledge of the game, and tried to give honest opinions. But somehow I didn't progress as quickly as I wanted. Neither did I get offered the regular work I needed. Maybe I wasn't as good as I thought, which is fine, but I couldn't help feeling that the BBC was discreetly, unobtrusively racist. Although Garth Crooks is still there, and has been for many years, I don't believe he is given the exposure he deserves. He's a cultured and erudite man who knows the game inside out. At Albion, he was reading *The Times* and had a well-defined cultural hinterland. I can't help thinking that he should have done more stuff for the BBC but, without quite being able to put my finger on it, I have a gut feeling that there's a streak of prejudice in the Beeb that holds back black people. Put it this way: I would rather be called a 'black bastard' by a fellow player than be subjected to the soft, low-key discrimination of the BBC, which is busy pretending it stands for one set of principles while actually practising something rather different. Simple as.

Three or four years ago, John Terry was accused of racially abusing Anton Ferdinand in a match between Chelsea and Queen's Park Rangers. Allegedly, he had called Ferdinand a 'fucking black cunt'. Months later, and only after being brought before Westminster Magistrates' Court and, shortly after, having to face an FA hearing, Terry was cleared by the one but subsequently banned for four matches by the other and fined £220,000 for using insulting words that included a reference to Ferdinand's 'colour or race'. It was a complete mess and involved a lot of unnecessary time and money. Terry should have admitted using the words, saying he used them in the heat of the moment (or whatever), but that didn't make him a racist. Everyone in the game would have understood the logic of the situation. I think Anton would have taken that, too. I believe that despite insisting on a comprehensive review, he told the investigating team that he was not actually accusing Terry of racism, merely of being called 'a fucking black cunt'. For me, Terry's offence was in running away from what he'd said and not having the balls to take what was coming to him as a consequence of making the kind of remark that is anyway heard quite often on a football field. Terry's response ensured that something that was understood in a footballing context resonated beyond the moment and was held up to scrutiny by other, non-playing institutions, such as the law and the FA, who – excuse me – know fuck all about the reality of actually playing top-class football.

But the thing that really pissed me off about the whole

palaver is that, in my view by allowing it to rumble on, Terry made the FA think they had to make a choice between him and Anton's brother Rio, who was Terry's partner at centre-back for England, for the 2012 Euros. Perhaps inevitably, the FA omitted Rio on supposed footballing grounds, even though most people didn't buy it and believed that he was excluded to avoid a potentially embarrassing situation. What a fucking surprise. The white England captain was retained at the expense of the black bastard. That's what I mean when I say the establishment doesn't do much about racism when it does actually happen. Not really. *Kick It Out* is a bit of joke in this respect and I can understand why, later, Rio refused to wear its t-shirt for the warm-up in a game against Stoke. Why the fuck should he? When push came to shove and there were chances to do something more than wear a fucking t-shirt or hand out fucking leaflets or whatever, they did sod all. On other occasions, Joleon Lescott and Jason Roberts have also refused to wear the t-shirts. I don't blame them. When they really have to get off their arses and make difficult decisions, British institutions usually take the easy option and preserve the status quo.

It is what it is, but it works the other way, too. I mean, when it suits the establishment to accuse someone of racism and claim a high-profile scalp, when it makes them look tolerant and inclusive, when it's easy to seem principled and high-minded, then the opportunity is grabbed with both greedy hands.

When Ron Atkinson arrived as the manager at Albion, my game improved no end and in a short time I became part of the first-team squad. That was because Big Ron was a fantastic man manager, by which I mean he knew how to get the best out of his players and he was able to get the best out of them because, by and large, they felt valued and loved by him. You can't fake that sort of thing – players soon rumble a fraud – and nearly all the players that Ron managed feel the same way. And that includes black players. At Albion, in 1979, he had three black players in his team at a time when it was unusual to do so: Cyrille Regis, Brendan Batson and Laurie Cunningham. Ron said, 'They could have been yellow, purple, and have two heads. So long as they could play and they were good lads – and they were.'

When Ron returned to Albion (from Manchester United) in 1987, those who were there in his previous stint spoke about him with misty-eyed reverence ('a great bloke', 'couldn't meet a nicer fellow' … that sort of crap) and predicted how well I would get on with him.

And I did. Straightaway.

He was larger than life, bubbly and with an infectious sense of humour. More to the point, he was honest, decent and straightforward. I have a very strong bullshit detector and I knew almost from the off that here was a man that could be trusted and whose bonhomie was neither false nor untrue.

A few years later, when I'd joined him at Sheffield Wednesday, we were in the final of the League Cup against United. We were in the old Second Division then and very much the underdogs, and part of the reason that we won 1-0 was because of Ron's ability to relax the team and make us believe in ourselves. He understood exactly what was needed and the players responded because they were devoted to him.

I was suspended for the final and in danger of showing

my arse, but Ron called me in and said, 'CP. This game against United. I need you to play the best game you've ever played.'

'But I'm suspended, boss.'

'I know that, you twat. I know that. But I still need you to play your best game. Don't go all mardy on me. I need you to be around the team and to be *you*. Understand?'

'Yes, gaffer.'

'Good. Now fuck off.'

'Yes, gaffer.'

But here's the point. None of the players, white or black or whatever, would ever have done anything for Ron if they'd even for a moment suspected that he was insincere or feigning his loyalty for and understanding of them. He was – is – one of the most inclusive, open-minded and genuinely warm-hearted blokes I have ever known.

But in 2004, during a Champions League game when he was heard to use racist language about the Chelsea player Marcel Desailly, believing the microphone was switched off, he was an easy target.

What he said was, '… he [Desailly] is what is known in some schools as a fucking lazy, thick nigger'. Although the comment was not broadcast in the UK, it was heard in the Middle East and then 'reported' to the press who, of course, made the most of it. Incidentally, Desailly himself doesn't ever appear to have had a problem with what Ron said. He's a clever and dignified man. He knows the game and he knows Ron, who – by the way – tried to sign him on a number of occasions. Despite being the unwitting butt of the ill-chosen remarks, I don't believe he's ever accused Ron of being a racist.

At the time, when asked by the BBC for a comment, I

said, 'I'm black and I'm sitting here and I'm gonna stand up for Big Ron not because he's a friend of mine, I'm standing up for him because I know what he's like as a bloke. If we're going to deal with racism then let's deal with the bigger picture of racism not about a throwaway comment that wasn't meant in that manner.'

I stand by that. Others lined up against him. One black player called Ron 'disgusting'. He resigned from ITV before they could sack him. *The Sunday Times* referred to him as 'Racist Ron'. He had to leave his job as a columnist for *The Guardian*.' Other newspapers said it wasn't the first time that Ron had used racist language. He was condemned by anti-racist groups, vilified by the public, and became a kind of national punchbag for all those who were rather too keen to advertise their liberal, anti-racist credentials. Ron had made himself an expedient focus for all kinds of fucking twaddle but the fact remains that he's no racist and hasn't got a bigoted bone in his body.

Meanwhile, the FA and *Kick It Out* were busy bottling the Ferdinand/Terry business. It's worth noting that the one is a sponsor of the other, and clearly wanted its captain to play for England. And, incidentally, Chelsea were also represented on the FA. Still, it was not and is not my business to make calls about John Terry, who almost certainly isn't a racist, but I can't help seeing red whenever I think about his situation compared to Ron's: one man lost his career while the other was allowed to continue. The BBC and authorities like the FA are the biggest hypocrites of the lot when it comes to racism. They are frightened to deal with anything that might be controversial or difficult or painful, only paying lip service to prejudice only when a convenient victim like Ron comes along and unintentionally makes their jobs simple. But real racism, by which I mean hatred with real intent, will always find a way to outmanoeuvre linguistic correctness, which is, let's face it, often complete balls, and why I never had a problem with players calling me a 'black bastard', so long as they said it in the right way.

4

Pushing Hard

'Home life as we understand it is no more natural to us than a cage is natural to a cockatoo.' George Bernard Shaw – *Getting Married*

I open my eyes and look round the bedroom. Seven-thirty. In the morning. *Sunday* morning. The previous night, I'd been to a Burns' Evening at a friend's house in Pudong, which is a suburb of Shanghai, located east of the Huangpo River. My own apartment is in Puxi, the historic centre of the city. For many years, I have abstained from drink during the month of January and even though I like drink and drinking, this time it has been relatively easy. Mind you, I am also looking forward to February 1st.

So. Seven-thirty. Soon I will get up and go to the gym. Despite there being no alcohol to sweat out, I'll still go and do my habitual ninety-minute workout. Rain or shine, drunk or sober, at home or on holiday, that's what I do. Always. Regardless of the fact that I will certainly go there, I do not particularly like going to the gym. I have been regularly not enjoying going to the gym for years and, no doubt, I will continue to not enjoy going to the gym for many more years to come. My gym gear is already laid out, neatly folded, waiting for me. So are the clothes I will wear after I have finished in the gym. Before I put them on, I will shave and have a bath (always shaving first). When I do dress, I will put on my clothes in the same sequence as always. And I will brush my hair in the same way as always. And I will apply aftershave the same way *as always.* Lucy will tell you that I am a slave to routine. She will tell you funny stories about the habits and drills and routines that I adhere to on a daily basis. But I do not see them as regimented behaviour, more as typical or normal behaviour.

I live on the twenty-first floor of a serviced apartment block. Several hundreds of feet below, the traffic on Huaihai Road is already quite thick. I am sure it is noisy down there – the Chinese love to sound their horns – but I can hear nothing. From my vantage point, it's like a silent film. Over the road, I can see Marks and Spencer. There are plenty of other familiar names (Gap, Starbucks, Muji) and up to a point I could be anywhere. The sky is gunmetal grey – though admittedly a dirty gunmetal grey – and I wonder what the pollution levels are like this morning. Usually, they are not as bad as the levels in Beijing and some of the other northern Chinese cities, but over the last week it has become relatively toxic. I have an itch in my throat.

Lucy is still sleeping. I reach out and touch her, not very gently, and she mumbles something. Probably something like, 'Fuck off, Carlton'. I pull back the duvet, sit upright, and pivot my legs on to the floor. Unlike many ex-footballers, I do not feel a twinge of pain when I do this. There are – fingers crossed – no taut hamstrings, no seized knees, no grinding cartilages. I am fifty years old. I walk without difficulty into the living room. It is not fussy or cluttered, not especially homely or cosy, but there are photographs of

Lucy's daughter and my children, a couple of books, some flowers, and the odd ornament. It feels like home. This is Lucy's doing. She is the one who applies the touches and creates a sense of domesticity.

All the same, I am the one who found and chose the apartment, making a video of it to show Lucy before signing up, but nevertheless wanting it and settling on it before she arrived. I like stability and I used the same criteria in choosing the apartment that I have always used when choosing where to live. Whether it's a training ground or a school, I don't like being a long way from work. I need to be close to transport; I don't want to feel isolated; and I must be close to the place where I do my banking.

The same criteria applied when I moved from Albion to Sheffield Wednesday in 1989. My first move. I'd been at Albion for five years and had no thoughts of a transfer to another club. One day, I turned up at the training ground and was told to report instead to the main ground, The Hawthorns. Two other players came with me – David Burrows and Steve Bull, also local lads. None of us knew what was happening. I had played for the England U21 team and was playing well – we were all three of us playing well – so I really wasn't prepared for what happened next. It crossed my mind that we were being disciplined for something. But what?

David Burrows was the first one into the office. He came out about five minutes later.

'What happened?' I said.

'I'm out,' he replied.

'Out?'

'Transferred.'

'Why?'

'We're skint.'

'Who are?'

'We are. Albion are. They need to sell us for the money.'

'Fucking hell. Where are you going?'

'Liverpool, I think.'

'What about us?'

'Fuck knows. You're next CP. Better go in.'

I went in and was told that Chelsea and Sheffield Wednesday had put in offers for me. Later, I talked with Ken Bates on the phone and even though he said that he was also in for Dennis Wise and wanted us to play together in Chelsea's midfield, I decided to sign for Wednesday. In some ways it must have seemed a strange decision as Wednesday were almost certain to be relegated. But Nobby Stiles said it was a 'no brainer' and that I should head north and join Ron Atkinson who (he said) was putting together a good team, reshaping the club for next year, and was aiming for immediate promotion. So I went to Wednesday for £750,000 plus Colin West, who joined Albion as part of the deal.

***

I'd had a good time at Albion. I joined them on a YTS (Youth Training Scheme), which meant I was behind others who were there on apprentice contracts. Although the first year or so was quite tough, I learnt how to prove myself and to be resilient. The youth team coach was a bloke called Ron Hodgkinson and he didn't pick me because I wasn't his player and, frankly, because he didn't like me.

At that time, I played exclusively as a centre back and, at times, the few times I did play, I was pretty shit. In one

game, I had been responsible for us conceding three goals
– before half time. Looking back, I can see that the setbacks
only made me more determined to succeed.

All the same, my confidence had taken a knock and it
was only when Johnny Giles arrived as manager – with
Nobby Stiles – that things changed for me. Nobby gave me
confidence. Perhaps he saw in me the same ungainliness
and determination that he had as a player. Neither of us
looked much like footballers, though we were pretty
much at opposite ends of the not-looking-like-footballers
spectrum. From worrying that my contract might not be
renewed and that I might have to become something other
than a footballer (maybe even a fucking postal worker) I
started to become strong-willed and almost perversely
resilient.

From that point on, failure and not becoming a
professional footballer were not options. I pushed myself
hard in training and began to establish the routines that
would ensure I got to where I wanted to be. Quite quickly
I was nicknamed 'The Freak' because of my fitness levels.
In my home debut as a full back against Birmingham, I'd
proved that I could hold my own against Robert Hopkins
and Kevin Broadhurst, who were testing me by constantly
switching wings. Bryan Robson, a boyhood hero who was
now a teammate, told me, 'Your game's about fitness.
Get yourself on,' meaning that I should find a way to do
whatever it took to *get on* as a footballer. It was about this
time that I saw in boxing, which I'd always been mad about,
a mind-set I could use about finding a way to win.

So there I was, playing with good players I had recently
idolized (players such as Cyrille Regis, Martin Bennett,
Alastair Robertson, and Derek Statham), developing

my game, finding a rhythm and a routine to sustain my improvements, living close to my family, getting married, and not even considering a move away from Albion.

No problem.

Immediately I arrived at Wednesday it felt like the right move. Ron did his trick of walking me out to the centre of the pitch and told me, 'If you get your head down and work hard, you'll play many times for England'. He did it so well that even had I known it was his custom to do this, though that didn't mean he wasn't sincere, I'd have still believed him and signed. Only when I'd been there a few weeks did I appreciate that financially I wouldn't actually be much better off than I had been at Albion. Nigel Pearson and Nigel Worthington, both a few years older than me, said I needed representation. They introduced me to David Plumber, who has since handled all my deals.

Still, it didn't matter. (Much.) I knew I was going to be happy at Wednesday and I liked Sheffield, its sense of post-industrial disrepair chiming with what I had grown up with in the West Midlands. I'd already sold the first house I'd bought and moved to my second property in Sutton Coldfield, and now I sold that, too, and bought a house in Lichfield, which was about an hour from Sheffield, straight up the A38. Ron didn't mind this as he also lived some distance away, in Barton Green, which is in Staffordshire.

All the same, I found that I needed routine and stability, and this started with needing to be close to the training ground – within thirty minutes, my psychological cut off point. Any further, even a minute further away, and I became twitchy. I also bought a flat in Sheffield. I needed to be close to the training ground because I trained twice every day, and sometimes in the evenings, too. Train, sleep, train, sleep, train. Buggering off back to Lichfield, even though it wasn't that far, didn't really work for me. I knew my game and I knew my strengths and I knew that I had to be fit. The Sheffield flat was just a place. It was home without being at all homely, a place that facilitated my professional requirements. I had it redecorated when I moved in, but that was about it.

It was here that I began to understand what it was I had been doing, perhaps without properly appreciating it, for several years at Albion. What it was that allowed me to develop as a footballer, and what I needed to reproduce in Sheffield if I was to make further progress.

Elite sportsmen need routine, sameness, pattern, repetition, drill, ritual, and habit. Their performances are grooved on the field of play by the predictable, controlled lives they lead off it. There can be no physical distractions, no tangible disturbances to this life of entrenched procedure. Having said that, there are of course a few notable exceptions, but for mere mortals, it's all about the preparation and the regime.

I've often wondered why this is so. I think it's because the replication gives you confidence and sport, at least at the very top levels, is played in the head. I know this is a cliché but it happens to be a true cliché. Most people, including me when I started out, believed that training was simply about practising skills and fine-tuning the body. Well, that's partly true, but it's also a way of preventing uncertainty and developing self-assurance, manufacturing a sort of inner strength that enables sportsmen to push themselves that little bit harder and have a kind of inner conviction about their level of performance. I mean, apart from a few naturally gifted anomalies, most footballers at the top level can kick a ball and run around a lot. The game isn't rocket science and everyone who plays it has two legs, a willing body, and a basic understanding of what is required to excel. You need something a bit extra to separate you from the many thousands of others who would jump at the chance to take your place.

It was at Wednesday that I consciously cultivated the routines that I knew were important to the kind of player I wanted to be. So I bought a flat that was twenty-eight minutes from the training ground. I organised and put out my clothes in the same way every day. If we won, I wore the same boxer shorts until we lost. I threw out clothes if I'd worn them and played crap. On match days in the changing room, my shoes had to be aligned *exactly* in the same place on the same bench. I would always come out of the changing room last and insisted on being the last one onto the field. There were two toilets in the changing room and I always used the same one. I always sat on the right side of the bus. And I would always have a brandy before each game. I would wander into the lounge area in the main stand at Hillsborough, past the surprised sponsors and besuited executives, jog to the bar where the bar staff had lined up my drink, swig it down, and run straight onto the pitch.

The need for stability and the obsessive seeking out of a sense of permanence has nothing to do, by the way, with a craving for home or one's roots. The desire for sameness is manufactured and doesn't depend on place. When I moved to Wednesday, I simply fabricated my own repetitious environment. Homesickness isn't an issue for a sportsman. You might miss people – I missed my family when I moved to Wednesday, even though Sheffield was hardly at the other end of the world from the West Midlands, but missing people and longing for home are entirely different things – but few of those who have chosen sport as a career are lonely or unhappy. At least, I wasn't lonely or unhappy. I was too busy focusing on my career. What was it Muhammad Ali said? Something like, 'If I can't beat me, then who can?' And rituals are a part of the focus. Almost all players have them. Gary Lineker habitually took Imodium before England games; at Albion, the goalkeeper Stuart Naylor was sick before each game; whenever I came across him for England, Stuart Pearce used to find a quiet corner, put on a set of headphones, sometimes even sticking his head inside a book. He didn't even do stretches before a game, his routine unvarying and deliberate. When Graham Taylor asked him, as England captain, to take the team for its pre-match stretches, Pearce gave him a withering look and said, 'I don't do fucking warm-ups'.

Quite soon after I'd joined Wednesday and moved into my unhomely home twenty-eight minutes from the training ground, my wife Jenny called. I used to go back down the A38 reasonably often but a heavy run of fixtures meant that I'd tended to stay in Sheffield most of the time. We chatted about various things, including the kids, who wanted to come and see me.

'That's fine,' I said. 'Come up on the Friday and after the game we can all go back to Lichfield together.'

'Will we all fit in your flat?' Jenny asked.

'Just about,' I said.

'Are you sure?'

Yeah. I think so. I'll be in a hotel, so that will gave you more space.'

'In a hotel?'

'Yes. In a hotel.'

'Why will you be staying in a hotel?'

'Because I always stay in a hotel before a match.'

'Even though we're coming up to see you?'

'Yes.'

'Why would you do that?'

'It's my routine.'

'You have to do it?'

'Yes. I do.'

'Fucking hell, Carlton …'

'Sorry. It is what it is, Jen …'

I couldn't find the words to explain why going to the hotel was so important to me. The same hotel and more often than not the same room. I couldn't explain to her how spending time there was part of the stabilizing process that allowed me to maintain the belief I was an elite performer with the resolve and resilience to give my best in the competitive world of top-flight football. Frankly, it sounded wanky. How could sitting in an anonymous room about twenty minutes drive from where I lived and where my family was staying have anything to do with my ability to function as professional footballer? All I can say is that it did, or I felt that it did, which is more or less the same thing.

Only a very few deviate from their routines or do not seem to have routines. Paul Gascoigne was one. He used to get on everyone's tits in the England dressing room, clowning around and making a nuisance of himself, especially to Pearce who sometimes looked as if he wanted to kill Gazza, though I soon worked out that not having a routine was actually part of Gazza's preparation, an exhibition of misrule and mayhem that was unfailingly repeated by him before every match. Chris Waddle was another who didn't seem to be as single-minded as the rest of us. Both of them in my opinion were geniuses.

A couple of early examples which actually contradict what I've just said about the importance of routine and sameness. The first, a cold day at Norwich. Someone had left some bottles of brandy in the changing room and after taking a swig, Ron liked it so much that he told us to finish the lot before we went onto the field. We did, and we were 2-0 up inside twenty minutes. The second, an away game at QPR. The coach was late and we were stuck in traffic. Ron told us to get changed on the coach and then to run to the ground through Shepherd's Bush. We arrived at Loftus Road about five minutes before kick off, almost ran straight onto the pitch, and were 2-0 up inside fifteen minutes.

Nevertheless, what I said about routine holds good. And Nobby was right: Ron was building a good team at Wednesday, even though we were relegated that season. I didn't regret going for a minute.

5

Chemistry

'When I moved to Sheffield … there were certain challenges: if you've got a name like Sebastian, you either learn to fight or to run.' Sebastian Coe

It was sometime in 1994. I can't remember the actual date but it must have been in the summer, probably just after that year's World Cup in the United States. Dave Richards, the chairman of Sheffield Wednesday came to see me. Actually, came to visit me at my house, which was unusual. Neither can I recall what kind of car he was driving, or rather in what kind of car he was being driven. Naturally there was a driver. I suppose the car must have been a Rolls or a Bentley or something similar. And even if it wasn't, that's the kind of car my memory associates with Dave Richards.

He'd arrived at the club a few months after me and had been made chairman soon after that. So in some ways, we had things in common, were bound by the same chronology, had turned up at Hillsborough at more or less the same emotional time – quite shortly after the Hillsborough disaster and just before Wednesday's relegation from the top league. I'm not sure if we sensed there might be some kind of bond between us (certainly it was never acknowledged) but looking back I'm aware that we felt like new brooms, representing a new start for the club. I think he made his money in engineering and the treatment of waste, but wherever he made it he had clearly made lots of it and was prepared to use it to help Wednesday. I know Dave has his critics – and when he left the club in 2000 it was in debt, facing administration, and doing poorly on the field – but I always got on well with him. So when he arrived in his Bentley or his Rolls whatever, his soft, pudgy face, ramshackle like an ex-boxer's that had been left to soak overnight, his features both composed and concerned, his expression both smiling and serious, I was pleased to see him.

The background to this meeting, I guessed, was the deterioration of my relationship with the manager, Trevor Francis, and the rumours that I was disaffected and would be leaving the club. Ron had left to become manager of Aston Villa in 1991 and Trevor had stepped up from being a player to become the manager.

I invited him in and we were straight to it.

'I don't want to go,' I told him. And indeed I did not. I loved Wednesday. I loved Sheffield. I knew then and I know now that the years there were the best of my career.

'This is my fucking football club,' Dave said, 'and if you want to stay, you're staying.'

'I want to stay.'

'Ok. So tell me what you want.'

And I did. A five-year contract, a signing-on fee, loyalty bonuses, and so on and so forth.

Dave sat there listening and nodding his head. 'That sounds ok,' he said.

'Don't worry about me, Dave,' I said, 'I'll see out the five years.'

'We'll get the contract drawn up and you can come in tomorrow morning and sign it,' he said.

'Just one thing,' I said.

'What's that?'

'I'll honour my side of the deal. But if you decide to sell me, you'll have to pay me up in full.'

'No problem.'

We shook hands and the next day I went to the club's offices and signed the contract Dave and I had agreed on. At that point, we both thought that it was good business – we both wanted me to stay at Wednesday and the paperwork reflected that.

Soon after, it might have even been the same week, I got a call from Trevor Francis.

'Carlton, I've received a couple of offers for you. You can go to Leeds or Villa.'

'I don't want to leave.'

'You should consider these offers. They're in everyone's best interests.'

'Obviously you don't speak to your chairman, Trevor. I'll see you at pre-season training.'

The phone call ended abruptly.

Within five minutes, Dave had called.

'He doesn't want you, Carlton.'

'I thought you said it was your fucking football club, Dave?'

Pause.

'He doesn't want you,' Dave said, this time more quietly.

'I'm not speaking to anyone until I get my money,' I said.

'My hands are tied.'

'A contract's a contract,' I reminded him.

I didn't want to leave Wednesday but Trevor made it clear there was no future for me at the club. The supporters thought I'd left out of choice but in fact it was out of necessity. And I'd be fucked if I didn't get what was due to me. So Wednesday coughed up, paid out my contract, a deal with Villa was agreed, and then Howard Wilkinson elbowed his way into the picture and persuaded me to sign for Leeds. Almost six years after joining the club, having enjoyed all of them, and possibly thinking I'd see out my career in Sheffield, I was on my way to a local rival. Such is football.

Trevor had left Queen's Park Rangers, where he had been player-manager, in 1990. He joined Wednesday as a player and although in the final years of his career, he was still bloody good. Like quicksilver, with two good feet, an acute footballing brain, an eye for goal, and surprising physical resilience, he was still a right handful at the age of thirty-six.

As a player, I got on with Trevor fine. As a manager, I did not get on with him so well. There was a tension between us. Although it took a while to come to the surface and find any kind of public expression, it was often if not always there, a kind of latent ill-feeling. Looking back, it's hard to see where the fault for this lies. I'm not even sure if fault-finding is a helpful way of considering what happened although there was undoubtedly fault on both sides.

At QPR, Trevor had probably been aware of the fact that he was perceived as a nice, pleasant man. He was, and is, a nice, pleasant man and sometimes overcompensated for this by wanting to be identified as a martinet, someone who was a stickler for authority and wouldn't let anyone take the piss. At QPR, this had caused problems when he'd forbidden Martin Allen to attend the birth of his first child because the date was too close to an important game. Allen went anyway and was fined and suspended by Trevor, something for which he was criticised.

Because he was naturally a softly-spoken bloke – the sense of gentleness emphasised by his slightly nasal blurring together of West Country and Brummie accents, his somehow boyish features, and a pair of sad, sensitive eyes – Trevor thought he needed to go in hard with anyone in the dressing room who might give him problems. Although I never considered myself a problem, there was no doubt that I had attitude, wasn't afraid of speaking my mind, and didn't give a toss if I ruffled feathers.

There was also, as I've already suggested, my habit of responding to father figures, blokes who naturally exuded authority. Thus far in my career, though there would be others, Ron had been one of these, so had Nobby Stiles, and so (of course) had my dad. It wasn't that I didn't respect Trevor or like him – I did and I do – but I somehow couldn't look up to him in the way he wanted. It was a case of him knowing what I felt and me knowing that he knew, this mutual awareness causing a kind of stubborn awkwardness. The unacknowledged wrestling match that started between us went on for a year or so, not helped by me occasionally behaving like a dick, until things came to a head with the move to Leeds.

One of the signs that things between us weren't right was when Trevor signed Chris Bart-Williams from Leyton Orient shortly after taking over as manager. Chris was a good player and a nice bloke but when Trevor announced, before a cup game against Forest, and without talking to me about it beforehand, that Chris would play in the centre of midfield and I'd be moved to the right-hand side, it all kicked off.

Or rather, I kicked off.

'You can't do that.'

'Yes, I can.'

'I play centre midfield.'

'You'll play where I ask you to play.'

'I don't like playing on the right.'

'I've seen you play on the right for England.'

'I didn't like it. It's not my fucking position.'

'Your fucking position is where I fucking tell you to play.'

'In that case I won't fucking play.'

'We'll see about that.'

'I won't fucking play!'

There was more of this, quite a lot more, though of course in the end I did play. Although I can be a dick I don't think I'm an arsehole. In addition, I understand that I'm a professional footballer and therefore under a contract that obliges me to play, and to play to the best of my ability, which I always try to do.

A few days later we were playing badly against Forest and going nowhere so I took matters into my own hands and told Bart-Williams to play on the right and I would revert to my position in the centre of midfield.

'Just fuck off out to the right, Chris,' is the way I put it. 'I'm in the fucking middle now.'

'What about the boss?' Chris said.

We could both see Trevor on the touchline, suddenly aware of what was happening and looking at me, possibly even shouting something.

'I'll deal with him,' I said. 'But for the moment, just fuck off out to the right. Ok?'

Mark Bright came over to me.

'CP. You can't do that.'

'I'll do what I fucking like.'

'You're a twat.'

'Bog off, Brighty.'

'Bog off yourself, you stupid prick.'

'You just fuck off up the fucking pitch and leave the fucking midfield to me.'

At the end of the game, Trevor was not happy. He took me to one side and told me it was his job to pick the team and tell people where to play. If I didn't like it, I could fuck off.

'We were better with me in the centre though, weren't we?' I said.

'That's irrelevant,' he said.

'No it's not.'

'I think it is.'

'Whatever. I know I'm right.'

'You always think you're right.'

I considered this.

'Not always. But I know my best position and it's not on the right of midfield.'

'If you don't like it you can fuck off.'

'Fuck off yourself.'

The wound between us never properly healed. It opened up a year or so earlier and had been festering ever since.

It must have been March, 1993, Trevor called me into his office.

'I have good news and bad news for you, CP. Which do you want first?'

'The good news, please.'

'The good news is that Graham Taylor has been on the phone to me. He wants you for the next England game.'

'So what's the bad news?'

'You can't play.'

'What do you mean, I can't play?'

'I can't allow you to play.'

'Why the fuck not?'

'Because we've got an important game a few days later. I need you for that.'

We did indeed have an important game a few days later. Sheffield United in the semi-final of the FA Cup at Wembley. For anyone associated with Wednesday, it didn't get much bigger than that.

I tried to see things from his perspective but didn't have much luck. Once I'd got my own handle on things, there wasn't usually much room for other people's ways of looking at things. Pigheaded I am, and stubborn as they come. I probably said some things I shouldn't have said. A few minutes later, I left the office angry and disenchanted.

It didn't help that Graham Taylor called the next day, confirming that I would start the game, an important World Cup qualifying match against Turkey at the Ataturk Stadium in Izmir.

'I'll tell you now, son. You're playing.'

'We've got a game a few days later. I'm not sure Wednesday will release me.'

Taylor considered this. All he said was, 'It's an important game, son. I need you to play. It's the World Cup.'

That was enough. I went to see Trevor.

'I'm playing for England no matter what.'

'It's one game, Carlton. You'll get other chances.'

'I'm not interested in other chances. There might not be another chance. It's the World Cup. I want to play and help us to qualify and then play in the World Cup itself. I'm playing.'

To his credit, Trevor listened to me ranting and blustering – the usual shit about playing for one's country being every boy's dream and the World Cup being the pinnacle of every footballer's career. This was my chance to cement my place for the competition proper, which was to be held in the USA the following year. I might even have said something about it being a story to tell the grandchildren. I reminded Trevor of his own England debut, against Holland at Wembley. At the time he was still at Birmingham and I asked him what it had meant to him. And what about playing the World Cup itself, which he had in 1982? He went quiet and I could see him thinking, starting to relent, possibly hating himself for being (in his eyes) soft, *giving in,* and betraying the uncompromising characteristics he'd identified as being necessary if he was to succeed as a manager.

I sensed his uncertainty.

'No matter what, I'll be playing against United. I promise you that. I give you my word. Just let me play for England.'

There was a bit more toing and froing, but I knew he would eventually give me permission to play. And that's exactly what happened. We won the game 2-0 with goals from David Platt and Gazza. I played well in a bruising match in front of 60,000 hostile Turks who threw bottles and coins onto the pitch. It was my kind of game – intense, physical and competitive. There was only one problem. At half time, Chris Woods, who was in goal that night, looked at me and said, 'Fucking hell, CP. What's that?'

'What's what?' I said.

'That!' he pointed to my left foot.

'Fuck me,' I groaned. 'Fucking fuck me.'

The side of my boot had been split by a tackle and there was blood gushing from a deep wound. I hadn't even noticed it, the adrenalin of the occasion blocking the pain. The team doctor gave me some stitches (I think ten of them) and I went out for the second half. But after the game, I knew there was trouble. When I took off the boot, the wound was ugly, deep and serious. A two-inch gash, deep and gaping, blood oozing from it.

'What will you tell Trevor?' Chris asked.

'Fuck knows,' I said.

In the event, I didn't have to tell him. The England team doctor phoned ahead and informed Trevor about the injury.

Understandably, he went berserk.

'You promised me you'd be playing against United,' he shouted.

'Look at my foot. I can't even train.'

'You're fucking playing on Sunday.'

'I can't.'

'Find a way.'

'What way?'

'I don't know. Any fucking way.'

Although I couldn't train, within a day or so I did begin to feel better. I asked the doctor at Wednesday what he could do and he said it wasn't ideal, but he could take out the stitches just before the game, block the wound, and then freeze my foot. And that's what he did at Wembley, arriving in the dressing room with his medical bag shortly before kick off.

'Are you ready, CP?'

'Let's just get it done.'

He unpicked the stitches, blocked the wound with antiseptic padding, and then said he would have to freeze the foot with an injection. What he hadn't told me was that the needle was a foot long. I mean, really a foot long.

'Size of the fucking cunt!' I gasped. 'Seriously!?'

He didn't even bother to tell me it wouldn't hurt or make the usual joke about it only being a little prick.

As the needle went in, and in, and then in some more, the pain was violent, stabbing, unbearable. For the first time since I was a kid, I cried, unashamedly howling and sobbing at the agonising discomfort. Other players told me later that I screamed the place down. Worse was to follow. In the warm up, I found I couldn't kick the ball. Actually, I couldn't even run.

'Fucking hell, Carlton,' said Trevor. 'I knew this would happen.'

'I'll sort it,' I said.

'How?'

'I don't know but I'll sort it.'

When I went back to the doctor he said the only way I could play would be if he froze the whole of the top part of my foot, which meant another injection. 'It won't be so bad this time round,' he said. But it fucking was as bad this time round and I yelped like a stuck pig all over again as another twelve inches of hypodermic were slowly, unpleasantly introduced into my foot. When the doctor had finished, the foot was completely numb. I tired to stand up but the lack of feeling made it difficult and, like Bambi on ice, I slithered and slipped. Then, by stages, I literally found my feet. It took a bit of getting used to but after a few minutes I had learnt to walk without sensation.

'How long will this last?' I asked him.

'Ninety minutes,' he said.

'Just have to hope there's no extra time.'

Though of course, inevitably, there was extra time and, in the short break after the first ninety minutes, I disappeared for another shot. This time, there was so much adrenalin pumping round me that I didn't feel the pain. Only after the game, which we won 2-1, did the torment begin and my foot began throbbing with incredible hurt.

Trevor came into the dressing room to congratulate us. I couldn't resist saying, 'Told you it would be ok, didn't I?' but I knew that I'd damaged our relationship. He smiled at me though it wasn't a fence-mending kind of smile. Nowhere near.

They say hindsight is wonderful thing whereas it's actually quite often a pretty shit thing. Looking back, I can see that I gave Trevor, who would have been naturally suspicious of anyone in the dressing room with a big mouth, anyone who wasn't afraid to speak his mind, anyone who occasionally went too far, i.e. me, reasons to be wary. Perhaps he decided that he'd finally had enough in the match at Queen's Park Rangers on New Year's Day in 1994.

We'd arrived in London the day before and went straight to the team hotel. Although it was New Year's Eve, I always – almost always – behaved myself immediately before a game. So in the evening, I was in my room, relaxing, watching television, ready to sleep.

The phone rang. It was Chris Woods.

'Me and Waddler are going out for a quick drink. Come and join us.'

'No. I'm all right. I'll stay put.'

'Come on. Just one. It can't do any harm.'

'Where?'

'Pub on the corner. Not far away. A quiet drink. Just one. That's all.'

I'd like to think I took a bit of persuading, but probably not. Ten minutes later I was in the lobby ready for one quiet drink, dressed in my tracksuit, which was bright blue and had the sponsor's name – *Mizuno* – cartoonishly and luridly displayed. Woods and Waddler were each wearing a shirt and a pair of trousers.

'Where are you two going?' I asked.

'Quiet drink, CP. Like we said,' Waddler replied.

'I feel a bit of a twat dressed like this.'

'You'll be fine. Just to the pub on the corner. Quiet drink. Just the one. Night after. It'll be empty.'

The pub was on the corner but it wasn't empty. It was packed. The landlord recognised us, then made a big song and dance of calling us over and saying that drinks were on the house. So I had a drink after which I said I'd head back to the hotel.

'One more,' said Woods.

So I did.

Then Waddler said he fancied going into town.

'No way,' I argued. 'We've got a game tomorrow.'

'Just to look at the lights.'

'What fucking lights?'

'Christmas lights.'

'I don't know …' I tried.

'Toss for it,' said Woods.

'Can't do any harm, can it?' said Waddler, and produced a coin. 'Heads you come with us. Tails you can be a boring cunt and go back to your room.'

The coin came down heads and I climbed into a taxi with them, fearing the worst, unable to stop myself joining in. We drove towards where the Christmas lights might well have been but stopped outside the door of a club before we reached them.

'What's happening?' I said.

'Just need to have a word with someone,' said Waddler. We piled out of the taxi to be warmly greeted by the doorman, the Norwich player Efan Okoku's brother, and were shown to a corner table, which had been reserved for us.

'Fucking hell,' I said. 'We should get back to the hotel.'

'One drink. That's all,' said Woods.

'I should phone the missus,' I said.

'In the kitchen,' said Waddler. 'It's quiet in there. They'll let you use the phone.'

So I went to the kitchen and called Jenny, who asked where I was.

'Tucked up in bed and getting some rest,' I lied.

I went back to the table where Woods and Waddler had lined up another round of drinks. I'd probably reached the point of no return by this time and started to enjoy the drinking. Another round was ordered. Then another. And another.

Eventually, Woods looked at his watch.

'Time to go boys,' he said.

'Where?' I said, slurring the one word I could manage.

'You'll see,' said Waddler.

'Hotel?!' I protested. 'Big game. Tomorrow.'

'Come on, CP. You're only young once. Besides, we're here. We're all in the same boat.'

'We'll look after each other,' grinned Woods.

That being so, I allowed myself to be persuaded. Too easily persuaded.

So we clambered into another taxi and drove to Tramps nightclub where we drank some more and danced a bit. Or rather, I danced a lot, conspicuous still in my blue *Mizuno* tracksuit. By 4 a.m. I was bombed, barely able to stand, and in a dreadful state. I climbed onto Woods's back as we finally left Tramps, partly because of high spirits and partly out of necessity because I had more or less forgotten how to walk. By some mechanical process I hauled myself atop England's current goalkeeper and we wobbled precariously out into Jermyn Street and the bright early morning sun. To my mind, even though my mind was in fact barely functioning, it still seemed a bit early for there to be so much light. Then, by degrees, I understood that the dazzling light was the result of flashbulbs going off, the paparazzi being out in force to snap Rod Stewart who was, apparently, also inside Tramps. This was what had lured Waddler and Woods to the club in the first place; they were always going to end up there.

Semi-conscious by this time, we made it back to the hotel where I was immediately sick. Trying to soak up the alcohol with food didn't work as I was unable to keep anything down. Somehow, I managed to make it to the team meeting at 10.30. Trevor was looking at me in a very strange way. When the team was read out, Woods and Waddler weren't named – they had failed fitness tests a couple of days ago. The fuckers always knew they would not be playing. If I could have sustained any show of anger, I'd have gone ballistic, but for the moment all I was concerned about was staying upright, getting changed, and walking in quite straight lines.

Once we arrived at Loftus Road, I reasoned that I should leave changing to the last possible minute, hoping that things would get better. They didn't. When, by some otherworldly process, I managed to get onto the pitch, I straightaway felt terrible and threw up in the dugout. Des Walker immediately saw I was in some distress, sidled up to me, put his arm on my shoulder, and said, 'Steady on, CP. You just follow Les [Ferdinand] around best as you can, and I'll do the rest.'

'I don't think I can tackle anyone,' I said. 'If I go to ground, I'll never get up again.'

'Just follow Les. Remember: stay as close as you can to him. I'll do the rest.'

After staying as close as I could to Les for the first few minutes, Les said to me, 'Fucking hell, Carlton. You ok? You stink of booze.'

'The way you're playing,' I replied, 'I don't need to be sober.'

Des then played brilliantly, effectively doing his own and my job. The worst moment of the game arrived in the second half when they turned on the floodlights. The sudden brightness dazzled me and for a moment I didn't know where I was. At one point, I was so disorientated by their brightness that I turned to face my own goal. My legs and my brain were by this point functioning independently of each other, limbs and intelligence tuned to different, mutually exclusive operating frequencies. 'Wrong way,' said Les. 'Here, as we're so close this afternoon I'll give you a hand,' and he gently turned me through one hundred and eighty degrees so that I regained my true bearings. The other thing I remember is spotting Woods and Waddler in the dugout, pissing themselves and giving me an extravagant thumbs-up.

After the game, which we won 2-1, Trevor came over

to me. His face was grim. This was no act on his part, no attempt to play the stickler. It was the real thing. His lips were welded together with contempt.

'You might be in a spot of bother, Carlton.'

'I was in my room all night,' I protested, without even waiting for any specific accusation to be voiced. 'Unless you've got pictures to prove otherwise …'

'Funny you should say that,' Trevor said. 'You're on the front pages on several newspapers. You appear to be on Chris Woods's back wearing a blue *Mizuno* tracksuit.'

Who knows whether or not this was the moment that Trevor determined that I was too much bother or that he had to make a stand? He didn't say anything at the time, and nothing specific about my future at Wednesday was ever said until the morning that Dave Richards arrived in his Roller or his Bentley or whatever. But the chemistry between Trevor and I – as manager and player – was out of kilter. All I know is that a few months after the game at QPR, I was leaving the club I always regarded as my home.

6

Disappointing Excitement

'Blessed is he who expects nothing, for he shall never be disappointed.' Alexander Pope

It's difficult to know how to describe my years at Sheffield Wednesday, which were almost certainly the best years of my professional life. While I was there, I could imagine being nowhere else. Yet always the expectations and the sense of contentment were qualified by the nagging realisation that at some point it would have to end. That was the nature of the game, which is about dreams and disenchantment. Even so, I could not allow myself to deny the hope that things might in my case be different.

Anyway, and as expected, Wednesday were relegated within a few months of my joining them from Albion. I prefer to think the two events are not related. Although we clawed our way to 40 points, we were relegated on goal difference as Luton Town survived. These days, relegation would necessitate the breaking up of a team, its obliteration hastened by money-hungry young men keen to stay in the top division and earn as much cash as they could in whatever time was allotted to them as professional footballers. You can't really blame them because that's what the culture these days demands.

Although we were disappointed at relegation, you only had to look round the dressing room to see that Ron was building a good team. So rather than moping about it and looking to leave, all the players were relaxed about what had happened and were upbeat when the manager took us all to Marbella immediately after the season had ended.

It seemed a little strange – these kind of jaunts usually reserved for pre-season or as a reward for some kind of achievement – but a free holiday was not to be sniffed at and we all duly packed our bags and looked forward to a week in the Spanish sun.

Ron, of course, had a reputation as a lover of the sun and is often associated with being tanned (not always by natural means) and jangling with jewellery that is easily glimpsed through his open-necked, unbuttoned-to-the-waist shirts. As ever, the image is not particularly near to the truth; I don't think I ever saw Ron wearing excessive amounts of jewellery and I certainly never saw him strutting around, torso on display, like some kind of out of place extra from *Saturday Night Fever*.

So there we all were in Marbella, lounging around on the beach, waiting for Ron, who had called a meeting. After a while, he strolled up carrying his trademark red briefcase, similar to the one used by the Chancellor on Budget Day.

He sat down on some kind of beach chair that had been placed there especially for him and waited for us to gather round, subjects in his court. He was enjoying the anticipation and sense of theatre, an old hand at sensing mood and then playing the moment with exaggerated and theatrical bravado. He looked at us, then lifted the red case onto his lap, opening it with an over-the-top flourish, relishing the suspense. He produced from it our passports, crammed them awkwardly into his hands, and held them up for us all to see.

'I'm telling you now,' he said, 'we're going to win the league next year and do it in style.' Despite the incongruousness of the situation – the beach, the gaudy displaying of our passports, the contrived melodrama, the comedy of a lobster-red Englishman perched on a foldaway chair – we were hanging on his every word, and he knew it. 'Anybody who doesn't want to be a part of it can fuck off now. If you don't want to stay at Wednesday and you don't want to be a part of the team I've put together, then you can have your passport now and you can fuck off back to England.' Silence. 'Anybody?' More silence. 'Well, gentlemen, that being so I am assuming that you're all on board and I'll put these back here.' And with that, he threw the passports back into the case and took out a wad of money. He gave the notes to Nigel Pearson, our captain, before closing the case with a purposeful, decisive show of resolve. 'If anyone gets locked-up in the next few days, you're on your own. Now fuck off and have a good time.' And with that, he got out of his chair and began walking back to the hotel he was staying in – a different hotel from the one the players were staying in; he didn't want to witness what was likely to occur over the next few days.

Ron gave us four weeks off before pre-season training started and by the time we arrived back in Sheffield there was already a buzz of excitement amongst the players and a sense that something special was about to happen. The manager knew this and began building on the goodwill and spirit he had already created.

On one occasion, immediately before the new season

was about to start, he called a meeting in the dressing room at the training ground, saying that he wanted us to hit the ground running. Then he started talking about our new away kit, producing it from nowhere, like some kind of conjurer, and then brandishing in front of us a familiar-looking yellow-gold shirt. 'I want us to play like fucking Brazil,' he said, 'so we might as well look like them.'

The first game was away at Ipswich, who were also fancied for promotion that year. We won 4-1 and although we didn't play like 'fucking Brazil', we played pretty well, at least looking a bit like them, and straightaway sent a statement of intent to all the other teams.

Life was good that year. Being in the second tier of the English game didn't matter because we were obviously going to be back where we belonged by the end of the season. As Ron predicted, and even though we weren't quite fucking Brazil, we were enjoying the ride. Not many teams could live with us and the sense of gratification this created was infectious. Nothing felt beyond us. Even when we played badly it was as if we were deliberately creating situations that would test us.

In one game, against Oldham, who were managed by Joe Royle at the time and were a good team themselves, we were 0-3 down at half-time and playing shit. I was also playing shit. I'd just come back from an England B game and in the dressing room at half time, while we were waiting for Ron to come in and maul us, Nigel Pearson launched into me, calling me a 'Big-time Charlie' and telling me that I'd better sort it out quick.

When Ron arrived, he was red as a beetroot and beside himself with rage. He stood in the middle of the room, barely able to speak because he was so angry at what he'd seen. His whole body was vibrating with fury and you could almost feel the outrage inside him, struggling to find a means of expression. Eventually, after what seemed like an age but was probably thirty seconds of escalating but unvoiced indignation, as if the score was in some way a personal affront, he started to pick up the tea-cups and hurl them against the wall. After a bit of this, he finally found the words he wanted to say: 'You've got yourselves into this fucking mess and now you can get yourselves out of it.' And then the colour drained out of him – he went from red to white in about two seconds – and he stomped out of the dressing room, slamming the door behind him with such force that the whole stand seemed to reverberate. Then we all started to speak at once, tearing into each other, shouting, sometimes screaming, calling one another the worst possible names, questioning our right to be called professional footballers, and then, when the time came, going out for the second half pumped full of purposeful loathing and remorse. We got the score back to 3-3 and then with a few minutes remaining, Trevor came on as substitute and scored the winner.

Later that night, in a pub called the Devonshire Arms, we were watching *Match of the Day*. The landlord was a Wednesday supporter and looked after us well, not only with drinks but by roping off an area, feeding us well, giving us a bit of privacy, and making sure we had a good view of the television. The game against Oldham was one of the featured matches and Ron was being interviewed, saying that at half time he'd had to change things round, modify his tactics, make sure we got a grip of midfield, take a risk up front, and so on and so forth – all the things he perhaps should have said but didn't. But the point is, it didn't matter. There was a spirit and sense of camaraderie that implied, without having to be formally stated, that we were all in it together. Like a family, but better.

At some point during those years, I bought a house in Sheffield. A fucking big fuck-off house. It felt the right thing to do because I felt so at home in Sheffield and at Wednesday. I felt comfortable in Sheffield. It was big enough to have stuff in it that I liked and small enough to feel as if it was a friendly and intimate place. It was also close to my place of work and gave easy access to virtually any part of the country. There was an airport at Manchester, too, so foreign travel was convenient. And although Sheffield was an industrial city, or had been an industrial city – England was busy becoming industry-free in the nineties – the countryside surrounding it was beautiful and easily reached. Later, I would take my kids horse-riding in it every Sunday, the horses and the walking becoming part of my routine, preceding the boozing, which was also a Sunday habit. One Sunday, being full of it and full of myself, I called Ron and he asked how I was: 'Good, thanks,' I said. 'I'm here in my mansion, drinking champagne, with my fucking expensive cars parked out front and a few acres of garden to gaze over. There's a white man washing my cars and another white man cutting my grass. Life couldn't be better.'

On the football pitch, things were also going well. We clinched promotion, as Ron had predicted, with a home win against Bristol City. Oldham and West Ham also went up and we took the third automatic promotion spot behind them. We were probably the best team in the league and maybe lost more games than we ought, simply by playing open, attractive football. It was the year we also won the League Cup against Manchester United, though as described earlier, this was a game I missed.

In the next few years we finished third, seventh and seventh in the Premier League, reaching both domestic cup finals in the 1992-3 season but losing each one to Arsenal. Plus I made my debut for England against Russia. The only professional regret was not making the most of our opportunity in the UEFA Cup in 1992-3, the reward for finishing third the previous season. Thinking it would be easy after thrashing a team called Spora Luxembourg in the first round, we fucked up against Kaiserslautern in the second. We really lost it in the first leg in Germany. After five minutes we were 1-0 up, then conceded a soft penalty. Soon afterwards, David Hirst, who had scored our goal, was sent off. Eventually, we lost 3-1 and though we had chances in the second leg, somehow we just couldn't find a way to get back into the tie.

Although Ron had left after our first season back in the Premier League, we were still a good side under Trevor, the developing tensions between us notwithstanding. We should perhaps have won more trophies, the loss of both the League and FA Cup finals to Arsenal in the same season being especially disappointing. In the League Cup Final we were inexplicably flat. Due to injuries and suspension, I had to play at centre back, which I was usually happy to do, though I think Arsenal preferred me being there rather than in midfield. They were the better side in a dreary game and beat us 2-1, one of the goals being the result of a mistake by me when I tried to take a touch to a ball across the box when I should have just hoofed it clear.

Something else about this match sticks in the memory. I believe it was the first time that European clubs used squad numbers and player names on their shirts. We were given individual numbers, which we retained for the FA Cup Final and its replay later that year. Although squad numbers became compulsory for Premier League clubs the next season and are now an accepted part of football, at the time it felt strange.

I don't know why it felt odd but I have thought about it off and on since that day and I think it's something to do with making players individuals rather than part of a team. Although I can be a wanker and sometimes a conceited wanker, I always wanted to feel part of a bigger whole, a team I suppose, and being told what number you were playing in that team (rather than being a given a personal number for the foreseeable future) was all a part of that. This may seem strange from a man who threatened not to play because he felt he was being played out of position, but (of course) I did play and there was never any real chance of me not playing. I suppose I needed to feel that I was playing *for* someone, that kicking a ball around meant something other than making money or whatever – that it had significance for supporters and some kind of wider community.

That was one of the reasons why I liked it so much at Wednesday. The size of the city, the passion of the supporters for their teams, and the sense of belonging … all these things were important to me. I understand that modern football is a business and that managers and players must move around, but I still think that if it's taken too literally then players will end up merely as strolling mercenaries.

As I am writing this, I am in Shanghai reading about Liverpool's fans walking out in the 77th minute of their home fixture against Sunderland. They were protesting about expensive ticket prices (£77) and the refusal of the Liverpool board to pass on the huge fortunes from television coverage to their fans via cheaper ticket prices. The perception is that everyone in the game is now greedy for money, including the players, who have in many cases lost the bond that used to exist between them and the fans. Not unrelated to this is the news that a number of top players have been lured to China by big salaries. Ramires and Teixeira have just moved to Jiangsu Suning. Other big-name players have already moved over here and Arsene Wenger has made the point that with its financial muscle, China could move a whole league of Europe here. The reason for coming here can be nothing more than money and sooner or later fans are going to get pissed off with players who are only money-oriented and are little more than soldiers of fortune. I mean, I live in the country and even I'm not sure where fucking Jiangsu Suning is. And it's not as if Jiangsu Suning is a household name. So the only motive for coming here is money.

Now, I like money. I like making it and I like spending it. And I also work hard to make sure people don't take the piss when I sit down to talk about money. But I hope that when I choose where I play football there is also, somewhere in the mix, an awareness of other things, which is why I wanted to sign for Wednesday despite the likelihood of them being relegated.

Cut to the FA Cup Final, also against Arsenal, a few months after the League Cup Final. We had signed Paul Warhurst from Oldham and bought him as a full back or central defender. Paul was a great footballer – very quick, with two good feet, and he read the game intelligently. Injuries meant that we'd tried him up front and, trouble was, he couldn't stop scoring. He discovered that in addition to his other qualities as a footballer, he could also finish.

When David Hirst, who'd been out for a while with injuries, was passed fit for the final, Trevor informed Paul that he'd be resuming his old position. Paul, however, had grown to like his striking role – scoring goals, after all, is very glamorous – and refused to play unless he was picked as an attacker. As a consequence, he was almost left out of the side. Having made the same kind of threats to Trevor when he tried to play me on the right of midfield, I don't have much of a leg to stand on, but I can't say that Paul was right – even though I understood where he was coming from. All the same, the numbering thing troubled me and I'd hate to think its implications – that players were more important than the team or the clubs they played for – are irreversible.

It sounds like a cliché, but when the teams walked out for both cup finals (actually, all three cup finals – the FA Cup Final went to a replay), the racket made by the crowd was like a wall of sound, waves of orchestrated, sing-along, raucous pandemonium rolling across the old stadium and into the tunnel, driving its way into your bones until it almost became a part of you. Like Ron a year or so previously, Trevor had taken us for a walk round the stadium to make sure we weren't overawed. Even so, it was difficult not to be overwhelmed by the occasion.

The replay had been delayed by 30 minutes because of an accident on the M1 that prevented many of the Wednesday supporters getting to Wembley on time. The first game had been a deadly dull affair, a boring stalemate, and both sides wanted to do better. The delay for the Wednesday fans only made us even more appreciative of their support. Although it was May, the previous night had been wintry and

Wembley itself, already showing its age, looked battered.

I don't know if the Duchess of Kent made it to the replay but before the first game, she'd shaken my hand and asked, 'You're going to Aston Villa, aren't you?' Her briefing had clearly been thorough and thoughtful but more to the point I was startled that she had remembered the information and used it. I said, 'I haven't made up my mind yet, ma'am.' But what I was actually thinking was, 'Fuck me, even the fucking Duchess of Kent knows that I might be moving on.' Actually, any move was still a year away, and I was still very keen to stay with Wednesday, but with the obvious tension between Trevor and I, rumours circulated, and people knew that Ron and I had history. Actually, as the two teams were walking out, the Arsenal manager George Graham had momentarily put his hand on my shoulder and said, 'I might be seeing you soon, CP,' to which I replied, 'I don't think so, George. London's not for me.' I mean, Arsenal are a great club and I like London well enough but could never imagine actually living there: the traffic, for example – fucking nightmare.

In both games, but especially in the replay, which was a good, open game, I felt the warmth from Wednesday's fans in an almost personal way. I felt grateful so many of them had shown the faith to make another expensive journey down the M1. Even though it was impossible to distinguish anyone in the crowd, I could see in the stands, in my mind's eye as it were, all the people in the city who had made me feel welcome in Sheffield since I arrived there; all the pub landlords who'd looked after me; all the journalists with whom I had good relationships; and all the supporters for whom success for Wednesday was so important. I was captain for the day and it was impossible to contemplate anything less than a victory.

Which, of course, never came.

Nor was I made captain the following season, which would be my last.

Sad as it was, Wednesday and I were drifting apart. I didn't want my time there to end and it was with disappointment that over the following months I watched the shadows envelope me.

7

The Beautiful Stuff

'After the first glass, you see things as you wish they were. After the second, you see things as they are not. Finally, you see things as they really are, and that is the most horrible thing in the world.'
Oscar Wilde

Jimmy Floyd Hasselbaink once said about me that I was the only player he knew who could booze and still play football. I'm not sure he's right about that – I mean, about me being the only one. There are others. Quite a few others. But it is also true that there are many who *cannot* booze and play. Still, the fact remains that I like drink and I like drinking. Moreover, if there had been evidence that boozing had had an adverse effect on the way I played football, I am pretty certain I would have stopped or at least modified my behaviour. But apart from one or two incidents, a few of which are described within these pages, I really believe that regular, controlled drinking and occasionally getting pissed did not hurt my career. I can't speak for other people. If drinking is a problem for them, then that's their problem.

I once talked to Gordon Strachan about the difficulties of combining the responsibilities of being an elite sportsman with drinking. He pointed out that everything bad that had happened to me had happened after I'd been drinking. I countered by saying that many of the good things that had happened to me had happened after I'd been drinking. There was, in addition, we agreed, a pragmatic solution: train every day and don't drink shorts.

My reasons for drinking are not very original, though why should they be? They are, broadly, an enjoyment of the social craic and a sense of fearlessness – of being able to do anything – which is somehow retained in my psyche when I am sober.

I was introduced, if that is the right word, to drinking at Albion, where several of the players were regular boozers and had left templates showing how it was possible for committed drinking and professional athleticism to co-operate. A great deal has been written about drinking cultures at clubs and there has been a ton of media scrutiny on those who have suffered as a result of drink, but I think I can honestly say, in my own case, that I do not regret the booze. By and large, I have taken more from alcohol than it has taken from me.

It's not especially insightful to say that drinking is often the result of an addictive personality and that sportsmen who live highly regulated lives are perhaps more likely to form habits than people from other walks of life. Thus, for example, in addition to drinking, many footballers gamble. Or perhaps, needing a fix, some gamble because they can't drink.

I used to gamble when I first arrived at Wednesday. It seemed like a natural companion to drink – you drink whilst you gamble; the more you drink, the more you gamble, the daring and risk-taking of the one being fuelled by the consumption of the other – but after I'd lost a fair amount of money (in the end, almost everyone loses a fair amount of money), I stopped. Actually, I didn't stop but *was stopped*. A man called Dave Allen, who also owned a nightclub called Josephine's, ran Napoleon's, the casino at which I gambled. One night, there was a misunderstanding about a late night drink after an away game at Ipswich. I said something when I should have probably kept my mouth shut (a recurring theme) and as a consequence was banned. It was probably the best thing he could have done for me.

There's a story about my drinking – there's always a story about my drinking – that in some roundabout way describes the way I feel about booze. By this time, I was playing for Southampton in what people call the twilight of their careers. I still lived in Sheffield and was catching a flight down to Southampton after a game against Leeds. I was travelling with Egil Ostenstad, a teammate at the Saints. He had been staying with Alfie Haaland, a fellow Norwegian.

It was still the morning and, as was my custom, I had spent Sunday boozing. The session had been a particularly long one and as a consequence I was still pissed when I boarded the plane. Thirty minutes into the flight, there was a resounding bang, like a muffled gunshot, and the plane lurched badly before steadying itself, albeit awkwardly. However, it was clear that something was wrong – it turned out that one of the engines had failed – and we were told to adopt the 'crash position'. Egil was whimpering. His wife was expecting a baby and he thought his life would end then and there. As we sat in the cabin, leaning forward with our hands clasped round our inclined heads, I started to talk to him. 'You're going to die, Egil,' I said. 'We're all going to die. You don't drink. You don't shag about. You've had no fun and you're going to die. Here, in this plane, your life will end. I don't care, Egil. I've enjoyed my life. Have you had a good time? I've had a good time. But not you, Egil. Sober, serious, sensible Egil. The end.'

The bloke behind us couldn't believe what I was saying and told me to shut up, which I did. For a few moments.

'It's the end of the road, Egil. Death,' I continued.

When we landed a few moments later, uncomfortably though without incident, the plane was surrounded by fire engines as it came to rest.

'Thank God,' said Egil.

'Sorry about that, Egil,' I chuckled. 'Couldn't resist.'

'No problem,' he managed to say, without being especially convincing.

But I thought about what I'd said to him. And I kind of meant it.

***

I'd played for England on Wednesday and a few days later played a hard league game for Wednesday. By Saturday evening, I was knackered.

Jenny didn't seem that sympathetic when I arrived home after the game, limping slightly, ready for bed even though it was still early. I didn't really want to talk to anyone and was looking forward to Sunday, when I could spend time with the kids and then, later on, get bollocksed.

'You're ok about lunch tomorrow?' she asked.

'What about lunch tomorrow?' I said.

'We've been invited out somewhere,' she continued, though I didn't take in the names of the people to whose house we'd been invited and didn't much care. I didn't want to go.

'For fuck's sake, Jenny,' I snapped. 'You know what I do on Sundays.'

'Can't you make an exception?' she urged.

And, in the end, I did make an exception, or rather I met her halfway. I agreed to the arrangement, and to spend whatever time it took to have lunch and hang around for the afternoon, so long as I could drink in the evening. We argued about this, as we increasingly seemed to argue about many things. At the time, it didn't take much to light the touch paper.

So the next day we trooped off for lunch, which was actually ok, and then drove back early in the evening, at which point it all kicked off again.

'You're not going out now, are you?' Jenny said.

'Of course I'm going out,' I replied.

'It's too late.'

'It's not fucking too late. And I want a drink.'

'You mean you need a drink.'

'Need? Want? Same thing. Actually, *want*.'

'I don't want you to go out.'

'Well I'm fucking going out. End of.'

'You can be such an arsehole.'

'You haven't seen anything yet.'

My argument, rehearsed many times with Jenny, was that the Sunday drinking was part of my routine, an aspect of the way I functioned as a person and a professional footballer. I trained every day, even if I'd been drinking, and (though there had been a couple of slips) never drank for the two days before a game, and was often abstemious for the whole week ahead of a fixture. But drinking on a Sunday reminded me of who I was and confirmed in my own mind that I was trying to have a good time – that I played football because I loved it and was not some kind of automaton, merely programmed to perform. I made plenty of sacrifices to play football at the highest level and this was one of the ways in which I prompted myself to recall that I was also a human being. And, of course, I fucking liked it.

A little later, while I was putting the kids to bed, Jenny must have sent our driver Noel away, probably in an attempt to stop me going out. More words were exchanged between us. Not to be outflanked, I decided to not only go out but to make a conspicuous show of going out. On went the white tracksuit and the sunglasses. In went the cigar. Slam went the front door. I drove off in the Range Rover with a can of Kestrel on my lap.

A few hours later, tanked up and way past the limit, I took a risk and got behind the wheel to drive home. Arriving at a junction, I slowed behind a taxi that had stopped just in front of me. Although I didn't feel a bump – the Range Rover was too well-cushioned to register anything less than a proper shunt – I had the sense of a slight impact. So I clambered unsteadily out of my car and asked if there was any damage. The taxi driver confirmed there had been a small collision. I think he had a passenger inside his cab. I already had a number of drink-drive offences and didn't want to be disqualified from driving, so I offered to pay him cash for any damage. He agreed and we arranged that I would find him and hand over the money tomorrow.

So far so good. But when he asked for my telephone number, something I never gave out, the mood changed and, probably thinking that I wouldn't make good my promise, he called for back-up. Within a minute, or so it seemed, four or five of his mates, other taxi drivers, had arrived. In a panic, and having somehow climbed back into my own car, I reversed the Range Rover onto the kerb, I think in the process hitting one of the reinforcement cabs but more or less skirting the small squadron of other taxis that had appeared, and drove home. I must have been three or four times over the limit so parked the car, bundled myself into the house, put myself to bed, and told Jenny not to let anyone into the house. Then I fell asleep.

The next thing I remember was the police turning up and being shown upstairs by Jenny. More than that, when they asked where I'd been that evening, she replied, 'I don't know. But he's been out.'

The police officers insisted I came with them and took me to the nearest police station. I refused all the tests they asked me to take – how could I do otherwise? – and when the intoximeter didn't work, they demanded that I accompany them to another station. They wouldn't allow me out until I gave a reading. That was when I discovered how far over the limit I was. In desperation, I called Jenny, who put the phone down on me. I thought about my next move and understood that I must contact Nick Freeman, a lawyer who specialised in finding legal loopholes that enabled drunk idiots like me to walk away from situations like the one I'd landed myself in.

Nick was based in Manchester so it didn't take him long to get to me. He looked at the evidence and talked to the policemen who'd brought me in. It all seemed very affable but I could see that two things were happening. First, that Nick was thinking very hard, listening with intent, weighing up everything that was being said to him, gathering information. Second, that the police didn't much like him. Or rather, were suspicious of him. They knew his reputation – already he was being dubbed 'Mr. Loophole' by newspapers, a nickname he has since trademarked – and were perhaps intimidated by his manner. Handsome, well-groomed, charming, and well-educated (he had been to a public school), the police were immediately on the defensive, even though he was apparently offering only charm and good-natured concern.

Nick sat me down. 'You're in the shit, Carlton.'

'How much shit?'

He considered the amount of shit I was in. 'Causing an accident. Leaving the scene. Failing to report the accident. Being in charge of a vehicle while more than three times over the limit. Driving without due care. Causing criminal damage. Refusing to co-operate ...'

'Ok. Ok. I get the picture. Deep shit?'

He nodded. 'Deep shit.'

'Go on ...'

'Three months inside.'

'Inside where?'

'Where do you think. *Inside*, Carlton.'

'Inside prison?'

'Yes.'

'Fuck me, Nick.'

'You've been done three times for drunk-driving already.'

'But three months inside.'

He looked at me but didn't say anything.

When the court case arrived, the press were there, waiting for me to be led away to the cells, my head hung in shame, perhaps with a tear or two welling in my eyes. It was a good story and confirmed in a simplistic way what many of the public wanted to think about rich, spoiled sportsmen abusing their privileged positions, getting above themselves, thinking they were better than everyone else, and not being the sober, responsible role models they were expected to be.

'There's just one chance,' said Nick. 'I'll ask one question and if we get the answer we want, you'll walk. If we don't get the right answer, I'm afraid it's probably jail.'

In court, there was a comical interlude about my identity, as I had not actually admitted to being the driver of the car at the time of the accident. The passenger in the taxi had merely described the driver as someone who was 'black and bald'. Then Nick called to the witness stand one of the policemen who had been involved in transferring me from one police station to the other after the failed intoximeter test. He asked him a series of apparently innocuous questions, asking the officer to read from his notes, then when he'd heard enough, he asked his one question. 'Did you read Mr. Palmer his rights?'

The policeman looked a little flustered.

'Yes, I did,' he said.

'I mean, did you read him his rights a second time, on arrival at the second police station, as the law obliges you to do?'

And, of course, he hadn't. Case dismissed. I walked away a free man, grateful but vaguely humiliated. I don't know Nick very well but I do know that he doesn't condone drunk-driving and sees his job as being able to offer the best possible defence to his clients, and if that means the police having to tighten up its procedures and it ends with better standards of policing, then all well and good.

Afterwards, Nick gave me a you're-a-lucky-man-and-don't-do-it-again speech, which was well deserved on my part and only made me feel even more remorseful – though deliriously and ecstatically remorseful.

However, I doubt that I will ever completely learn my lesson. I am flawed and fallible, flesh and blood, for good and bad. But I did make a couple of mental notes, one of which was a reminder to myself not to be such a prat again. The other note I made concerned the moment when the police arrived at my house and were shown in by Jenny; I decided that at some point I would leave her.

8

This England

'A thin grey fog hung over the city, and the streets were very cold; for summer was in England.' Rudyard Kipling – *The Light That Failed*

Although we are quite settled in Shanghai, more than settled because it is a great city, there are occasional moments of homesickness or longing for England. Lucy is probably more susceptible than me but we both miss our kids – even though they're grown-up – and our families. My dad is ill and is getting on, so for me the sense of aching is complicated and heightened by anxiety and the thought that I might not see him too many more times. But I also miss the countryside, especially the countryside around Sheffield, which I have grown to love. I like walking in it and looking at it and driving through it. I just like being in it and near to it. There are other things I miss, too. Pubs, obviously. And certain foods. But also the rituals of English life. The most important tradition for me is still Saturday and its association with football. Although these days the games are generally spread over two or even three days to accommodate television, it all starts on Saturday and I still get the same buzz I used to experience when I was playing or managing.

When I was a kid, I saw an old black and white documentary called *The Saturday Men*, which was about the place that football occupied in the country's psyche. I can't remember where I saw it or why. Maybe it was at school because the team that the film focused on was Albion. But the thing I most remember about it was the way that everything seemed to stop on Saturday for football. In the morning, people anticipated the game. In the afternoon, they went to the game. And in the evening, they went to the pub and talked about the game. Another striking thing about *The Saturday Men* was that the players often joined the spectators for a post-match pint and a game of darts. There was a sense of community about the whole thing, something I experienced at Wednesday, which is probably why I enjoyed playing there so much.

Although I can watch games on the television or at a sports bar in Shanghai, even the earliest ones don't start until around 9 p.m., so the feeling of excitement isn't quite the same and there isn't the same rhythm of expectation.

Hard as I try to not find it odd, which is probably not very hard, I still can't help finding it strange to walk into a bar and see a group of Chinese men wearing, for the sake of argument, Manchester United shirts (and it usually is United), with favourite players' names displayed on their backs. The problem isn't that they are Chinese but that the scene is somehow out of sync with its British counterpart. You'd have thought that a bunch of blokes wearing shirts and watching football would be the same anywhere, but it isn't. For a start, there's no banter. Nor is there a great deal of alcohol being drunk so there's not much of a boozy buzz. And whilst watching a game, they make the wrong sounds at the wrong time, as if they're experiencing a match in a different way. A goalmouth skirmish, for example, which might result in a shot going wide, would prompt a rapid series of instinctive, politely choreographed comments: Tsk! Ayuh! Ooh! Ah! *Eehyahah!* There are regular cries of 'Suit! Suit!' (shoot) and *'shou-qiu'* (handball). In an English pub, the same action would be met either by ragged roars of dismay and frustration or a delayed holding of collective breath until the final moment, at which point there would be an intensely emotional release, an exaggerated howl of angry, almost personal anguish. It's the difference between observing and being emotionally involved, as if your very life depended on what was happening. It's the difference between a game being an entertainment and stirring something irrational and madly relevant inside you.

I am not saying either one is better or more appropriate than the other but this kind of thing reminds me that I am English and possess an English sensibility about football and probably about many other things besides. I live in China, my parents are Jamaican, and I am black, but I am unequivocally English. Every day and in all kinds of ways I am reminded of this. So when I won my first full England cap I was proud as anything, not just in a professional way at having merited selection, but because it meant something to me. I, Carlton Palmer, had been chosen to represent my country. The word 'represent' is very important to me because it suggests that I was in some way symbolising or epitomising England. It's more than just a football thing. It's as if the person, the very thing you are, is somehow being authenticated, endorsed, exaggerated, and magnified. Carlton Palmer is England and England is Carlton Palmer. It just makes you feel *bigger*.

I have always maintained that the England manager should be English. If we can't find anyone good enough then we should still appoint an Englishman and use the situation to take a long hard look at what it is we're doing wrong. If I hadn't been selected for England, would I have been happy to play for Jamaica? The answer is probably 'yes' because Jamaica is in my blood. But let's say it was discovered that I had, for example, Belgian or Irish ancestors and the possibility existed of me playing for them. That is, of playing for a country for which I felt no genetic or cultural allegiance. Could I have played for one of those countries? The honest answer is that I am not sure. As a professional footballer I suppose I would have been very tempted to become an international player no matter what the circumstances. But as an Englishman, I really don't know how I would have felt. And what if one of those teams had played against England?

Anyway, this was not a conundrum I had to solve. I had represented England at all levels, including U21 and B teams, so in many ways this was a natural progression. Indeed, I had been playing very well for a while and was in point of fact a little disappointed not to get the nod before I did. While I was at a party, Trevor Francis told me that I would soon be receiving a call from Graham Taylor, who duly phoned, congratulated me, and said I would not only be in the squad for the friendly against Russia in Moscow but would certainly be starting the game. Harry Maney called me, wished me well, and said, 'It might be England but it's still eleven versus eleven, The same pitch. Just do what you do but be spot-on when you do it'.

I arrived for the first training session at Burnham Beeches, which is just outside London and is some kind of conservation area. At the time, I was sponsored by Ford and was driving a blue Ford Escort with the words 'Carlton Palmer' gaudily emblazoned along the side of the car. The bloke at the entrance to the car park stopped me and asked who I was. I wound down the window and pointed to my name. 'Can't you fucking read, mate?' I said. In the car park itself, I was aware of the other cars being more expensive than mine, *better*. The Bentleys and Aston Martins put my jalopy in the shade, though rather than feeling embarrassed I thought it was funny.

Having said that, I don't want to give the impression that I was overawed or felt out of place. I didn't.

Through playing for the England U21 and B teams, I was used to the protocol, which was replicated through the various levels, even down to the handing out of the kit. I also knew all the players, a couple of whom (Chris Woods and Des Walker) played with me at Wednesday. So none of that was a problem. And nor was there any kind of psychological issue about deserving to be called up or meriting a place in the team. I knew in my own mind that for a year or so I had probably been the best holding midfield player in the country so, without meaning to sound arrogant, I had been anticipating the promotion for several months.

Now, I know that there are people out there who don't think I should have been an England player. Last week, I watched a television programme apparently describing the worst players to have been selected for England. I was one of the players they settled on. A group of non-footballing ignoramuses – most of them comedians, actually comedians whose names I didn't recognise – spent an hour talking about a game they didn't understand and about players they didn't know. Their brief was obviously to be entertaining and, to an extent, though only an extent, they succeeded. It's quite easy to be amusing when you are doing not very much apart from being critical and finding fault.

Naturally, I understand that I am not everyone's idea of what a footballer should be. In this regard, my greatest strength – my physique – is also the thing that makes me most vulnerable to criticism. The spider-like legs, the gawkiness, the gangling gait, the flailing windmill arms. Believe me, I've heard it all. *The Freak.* Remember. People these days like their footballers to be pleasingly in proportion, to somehow look the part as well as being the part. I often wonder if Nobby Stiles would have been so warmly clutched to the nation's bosom had England not won the World Cup. And how would Bobby Charlton's comb-over parting have played with the hair-literate football crowds of the twenty-first century? Would he have had to endure the same abuse that Wayne Rooney experiences on a more or less weekly basis and which may have had something to do with his very public hair transplant?

Nor am I the most skillful or elegant football player in the world. I know these things and knowing them has always been a feature of my game. Mentally, I consistently had to push myself, to make adjustments against good players, to find ways of being effective against footballers who were more technically gifted than me. It's been suggested that this was actually an advantage because others didn't think I could play and therefore underestimated me. There might be some truth in this but I could play *well enough*. Chris Waddle often told me that I was a much better passer of the ball than people gave me credit for. Waddler was a piss-taker but I don't think he was taking the piss in this case. Ron Atkinson used to say about himself as a player that his second touch was always a tackle; that is not me. While self-knowledge and being realistic about one's weaknesses are an important aspect of being a professional footballer, I never saw myself as being technically poor, just not as accomplished as some others.

And it was Ron that gave me belief that I could play a bit. He signed me three times (and it would have been four if I'd gone to Villa rather than Leeds), frequently reminding me that whenever I arrived at a club, the results picked up. He thought the weakest part of my game was my finishing and that I should have scored more goals. But he never stopped encouraging me, and was always quick to pass on other players' compliments about me. 'Hey, CP. Ray Wilkins says he's bloody glad he doesn't have to play against you every week.' 'Carlton – Andy Townsend just told me it was like playing against two Carlton Palmers. What a fucking thought!'

And I came up against some of the best players in the world when I played. One of them, the Chelsea player Gianfranco Zola, said after a game in which he was virtually anonymous, that if I man-marked anyone they wouldn't get a kick. Competing against evidently superior technicians was the kind of challenge that drove me on. I think the most intimidating footballers I faced were in the Dutch team that included players like Ruud Gullit, Marco van Basten, and Denis Bergkamp, and not just because they were incredibly gifted footballers. Most of that Dutch side were also big. Very big. Gullit was a monster of a man, tall, wide, muscular and glistening with muscle-tone. Like a racehorse, in fact, though somehow and at the same time, graceful and poetic in the way he moved. In the World Cup qualifier at Wembley, which is a large pitch, he hit with minimal effort a diagonal ball from one touchline to the other. It was achieved with such little apparent exertion, the ball travelling like some kind of missile, with precision and power. When you saw that kind of thing, you couldn't help thinking, 'Fuck me, Carlton. You'd better be on it here.' Gullit was injured and was substituted at half-time. After the game, he brought me his shirt and told me that I'd given him a very difficult time. I wasn't especially aware of this but it was a gracious thing to say. And incidentally, Dick Advocaat, the Dutch manager, said I was the best player on the pitch, so I must have been doing something right.

There's a moment in a game against Manchester United that I like to think sums up what I'm about as a footballer. Cantona receives the ball and I close in on him. He then flicks the ball over my head and I spin round, uncertain where the ball is and wondering what's happened. As I recover my position and close down Cantona again, he does more or less the same thing, lifting the ball over me for a second time and causing me to rotate once more, my eyes wide and swivelling like something out of a *Tom and Jerry* cartoon, attempting to locate the ball. The whole episode made it seem as if he were somehow orchestrating my baffled movements, as if I were a puppet. But by the time the ball comes down again, I have worked out what's happening and manage to get in a block before he can properly get his shot away. His face, previously alert and mischievous, then sags with disappointment. The whole incident lasts maybe a couple of seconds. For much of that time, Cantona, who is supremely gifted, makes me look like a twat. But in the end, I do what I'm there for – to somehow stop him playing. All teams need a player like Carlton Palmer. That's why managers kept picking me. That's why

I won eighteen England caps. That's why I am one of the least substituted players of my position in the history of the Premier League. That's why, for most of the time, I left it to others to decide how good I was. Though as I get older perhaps I feel the need to say something to the uninformed wankers who offer their opinions in programmes like the one about England's worst players. And 'fuck you' is what I want to say.

***

When I first played for England, I used to room with Gazza. After matches at Wembley, the team had the choice of being put up in a hotel for a night or two or, if players preferred, being flown or driven back to their homes. After one game in which I'd roomed with him, I decided to stay on and invited Jenny down to watch a show and do some shopping.

I already knew Gazza from playing against him so I knew what he was like. A genius is what he was like. Gazza and players such as Lionel Messi are able to travel faster with the ball than without it. Strong on the ball, he had great skill, was audacious, possessed keen footballing intelligence, and just loved to play football. His enthusiasm was infectious and he brought to the team a sense of daring and fun.

Of course, I'd also heard all the stories about 'mad Gazza' and these are well-documented. But on this occasion, when it became evident to him that I didn't know London so well, he decided to take matters into his own hands.

'I'll look after you, CP,' he said, 'and make sure you and the missus have a good time.'

'How do you mean?' I asked, knowing that Gazza had

a reputation for playing practical jokes.

'You just leave the arrangements to me. Just relax, man.'

So, as far as I was able, I tried to relax. Jenny arrived. We settled into our room, did some shopping, and waited.

At about 7 p.m., we got a call from Reception saying that our car had arrived. When we reached the lobby, we were told that actually getting into the car would involve a short walk.

'Why's that?' I said.

'It's too big for the hotel car park,' replied the concierge. 'In fact, it's so big, it can't even make the turning into the car park.'

So Jenny and I set off down the Bayswater Road, keeping our eyes open for a big car. The vehicle that Gazza had organised for us was a stretch limo, though not any stretch limo, but possibly the longest stretch limo ever. Inside, there were flowers and champagne. The driver took us to a West End show and waited for us after it had finished, then drove us back to the hotel, or as near to the hotel as he could get before depositing us onto the pavement. I took out my wallet.

'How much do we owe for the evening?' I said.

'All paid for,' the driver grinned, and drove off into the night.

On another occasion, I came into the room we were sharing and Gazza was on the phone, obviously to a woman, with whom he was having a lewd and familiar discussion. Immediately, I sensed the need to give him privacy and signaled that I'd give him and whomever it was on the other end of the line a few minutes by themselves. So I left him to it, went for a quick drink, which lasted about fifteen minutes, and then went back to the room.

Gazza was still on the phone, still talking in the same intimate and vulgar way. I gave him a quizzical look, wondering whether I should make myself scarce once again. He looked up, waved his hand at me, effectively beckoning me to stay, and mouthed, 'Almost done'. A couple of minutes later, and after some fond farewells to the girl on the phone, he handed me the receiver and said, 'It's your missus, CP.'

And, of course, it was.

I tell these stories because Gazza has not had such a good time recently and although there has been some sympathy for him, the kind of sympathy that shades into pity, there's not been much understanding. For the media, Gazza fits into a particular mould, the Fallen Hero mould, whereby a man is built by journalists into a hero, after which he becomes a victim of his celebrity and comes crashing to earth. It's a story that sells newspapers and is easy to tell, so much the better if it involves drink (which in Gazza's case, it does) and/or violence (which in Gazza's case, it does), and/or eccentric behaviour (which in Gazza's case, it does).

But Gazza is simply a very generous bloke, a free spirit to boot, who happens to at the same time be a fantastically talented footballer. The media expends a great deal of energy bemoaning the lack of characters in the game but when they get one, they take a kind of gleeful pleasure in building him up and then knocking him down. For them, it's a story with longevity, narrative development, and an unfolding sequence of enthralling chapters. Most of all, it's a story over which the media has almost complete control.

I am very aware of all this – perhaps over-sensitive to it, in fact. Other than talking to the media before cup finals, which is expected of players, and then putting money into a common pot, I have never taken money from journalists or courted them. Apart from Alan Biggs, who writes for the Sheffield Star, and whom I have grown to trust, I don't talk to them.

Sometimes this has been perceived as being uncooperative or rude, and is probably one of the reasons why I am considered fair game for hacks who take the piss out of my England career. If we'd won things, I'm pretty certain that I'd be looked at in the same way as Nobby Stiles or perhaps John McGovern, the unfashionable midfielder that Brian Clough took with him to most of the clubs he managed. But we didn't win anything; I didn't make friends with the press; and I looked the way I do and played the way I did. From my point of view, not a winning combination.

***

On 17th February 1993, England played San Marino in a European Championship qualification match. We needed goals (everyone needs goals against San Marino) and I was given the job of holding the centre of the pitch, which would allow the other midfield players to get forward and support the recognised strikers.

Despite winning 6-0, we didn't play especially well. Gazza was oddly quiet, almost sullen, as if he was preoccupied, his mind wandering. Alan Shearer, who could have been relied on to score goals, was injured. And John Barnes was returning after a long absence through injury. Barnes was actually jeered by the England supporters every time he touched the ball. Although I am normally focused and therefore oblivious to crowd noise, especially at Wembley where the crowd is further away from the pitch, the booing was pretty obvious. Barnes was clearly affected by the near-racist nature of the abuse and the entire evening became something of a chore. We made hard work of winning, so much so that at one point I'd had enough of holding the midfield – holding it against what, exactly? – and galloped forward to get on the end of a cross, stooping low to head in my one and only international goal. That was in the seventy-eighth minute.

It should have been something for me to savour but the media has tarnished even that moment. In a television documentary about England, the one that painted such a damning portrait of Graham Taylor, rather than celebrating my goal he turns to his staff and the other players on the bench, and says, 'What was he doing in the fucking box? Didn't we tell him to hold the middle of the pitch, eh?' Without context, in particular the context of humour, his remarks sound churlish and make my goal seem as if it was scored almost against orders.

Straight afterwards, I happened to catch Jimmy Hill and Terry Venables talking about the match on television. Hill remarked that 'Carlton Palmer had a good and energetic game and I won't have anything said against him'. The implication was that Venables had said something against me – the two of them were often quite combative in their comments – but more than this, he (Venables) could be heard chuckling and guffawing at Hill's observation. It was a trivial moment but I knew then that if ever Venables became manager of England, I would be in trouble. It wasn't merely that he laughed, but there was something about the way he laughed – off camera as if playing to the gallery, with a kind of knowing smugness – that upset me.

Looking back on that game and the way my contribution

was put through the media mincer, both in the documentary and the post-match comments, I began to understand how public opinion is formed and how popular belief is shaped. I scored a goal for my country; in the long run, it worked against me.

If Gazza was the Fallen Hero and I was the Clown, then Gary Lineker was very much Prince Charming. He was more or less untouchable. I don't have a problem with this – Gary is a genuinely nice bloke and was a great player – but he also, like Gazza and I, slotted neatly into a prescribed media type. Well-groomed, boyishly handsome, smooth, articulate, courteous, presentable, uncontroversial, and he scored goals for England – the media loved him and before he finished his playing career he was being groomed for another in front of the camera.

Thus, when Lineker made his final appearance for England, during the 1992 European Championship game against Sweden in which, notoriously, he was substituted by Graham Taylor after 64 minutes when England were chasing a game they had to win, the press took sides. Lineker was left one goal short of Bobby Charlton's all-time record and the media had been robbed of something it liked to do – create a hero. Taylor was the villain, not only for denying Lineker and the whole nation the chance of bathing in the reflected glory of that moment (had it arrived) but also for wrecking the country's chances of progressing to the semi-finals of the competition.

The fact is, we were knackered. There had been a couple of hard fought draws before the Sweden game and all the England team had only recently completed an arduous season of Premier League football. Although we started the game well and scored an early goal through David Platt, there was no doubt we were running out of energy. The Swedes were full of running and we were in danger of being overwhelmed.

When Taylor brought on Alan Smith for Lineker it seemed in many ways a logical thing to do – we needed physical presence. And even if it was the wrong call (because Lineker's speed always threatened goals), the manager made the decision in good faith.

But the press thought differently and went for him in a particularly nasty way. *The Sun* ran the now infamous turnip head story and suggested that relations between Lineker and Taylor were so bad that team morale had been badly affected.

The misgivings I had about the media after the San Marino game, and in particular the way it could influence opinion, seemed more real than ever. In pitching Lineker against Taylor there was always going to be only one winner. Taylor was being cast as another media stereotype, the Pantomime Villain.

Taylor was in fact a genuine and thoroughly decent man who once admitted to me that in the early days of being a manager he had to gear himself up to use the muscular obscenities of the footballing world. Up to the point he became a manager, he rarely used bad language. His manner with the players was one of a kindly and concerned schoolmaster who knew our vanities and soft-spots, and who understood when to give praise and when to administer a bollocking.

At Watford, players were contractually obliged to do seven hours of community work every week. Taylor didn't insist on this just because of the community (though this was a factor – and Vicarage Road felt like a family club at a time when hooliganism and violence had a grip on the game) but because he was concerned with the wellbeing of his players. He wanted to develop them as individuals so that when the game spat them out at the ends of their careers they didn't blunder into the world like shipwrecked adolescents.

There wasn't a bad bone in Taylor's body but the media had shifted the narrative so that he was a step away from being perceived as the devil incarnate. Worse. The sort of devil who provoked laughter and derision. I thought at the time, 'If they can do that to him, fuck knows what they'll do to me if they decide to have a go'.

Playing for England was great. But it came with a health warning.

9

Hindsight

'Do I not like that.' Graham Taylor

Lovely bloke, Graham Taylor. And in so many ways. I can't speak highly enough of him – honourable, hardworking, honest, and straightforward. Normally a sentence like that has a 'but' attached to it, but in this case that's not going to happen. Like all managers he made mistakes – I'll come to those in a minute – though these don't detract from the basic truth that he was a decent man and a decent manager who was for the most part just unlucky.

Ron Atkinson always told me that managerial success was often a case of luck and timing, and if Taylor had little luck he had also taken the England job at a bad time. The 1990 World Cup semi-final team started to break-up almost as soon as the competition ended and continued to disintegrate in the following years.

By the time we were trying to qualify for the 1994 World Cup in the USA, Taylor was managing a generally inexperienced team. His style of management was also better suited to club football. He liked his teams to play functional football where everything done on the pitch was set up and rehearsed beforehand. You simply couldn't do that in international football where players and manager came together infrequently.

All the same, we were very confident of making the World Cup when the qualifying started. The group was a tough one (the Netherlands, Poland, Norway, and San Marino) but we were favourites along with the Netherlands to qualify. We recovered from an unfortunate home draw against Norway, who equalised in the closing stages of the game with a wonder strike, to put together some good results.

One of the peculiar things about the game was Ian Wright's continued inability to replicate for his country his club form for Arsenal. Wright was prolific for the one and shot-shy for the other. No one quite understood why this should be so and his potential to score goals would have been valuable to England, which was why he was given a number of chances to find his feet. But one of his strengths at club level was an ability to spark his own audacity and confidence by getting up people's noses. This was based on a knowledge and familiarity of other players and teams that wasn't available to him at international level. With Wright, it all started in the tunnel before a game – the cursing and the insults that were designed not just to wind up opponents but also to jump-start his own cheeky genius. The chat and the banter continued on the field and made him a fucking nuisance to play against.

Playing for Leeds, I remember we were winning 1-0 and Wright came up to me and said, 'Listen, C, I'm having a fucking nightmare but you know I'm going to score the equaliser, don't you?' And ten minutes later, he did. But he couldn't replicate this in internationals and was altogether a much quieter and more peripheral figure. Against British players or players with whom he was familiar, he was confident of himself and found a way of expressing this; it was almost as if he didn't have a language for international matches. Repeatedly calling a Turk a cunt, for example, might lose something in translation so, by and large, he didn't try to call a Turk or indeed anyone else a cunt.

Gazza was similar except he wasn't put off by the language barrier and just bashed on regardless. He and Wright were very different in the deployment of their otherwise similar tactics – Gazza was unselfconscious and took a child's delight in performing and playing. He also had a primitive and expressive set of mimes, which he would habitually employ, mostly to do with insulting an opposition player's looks or lack of personal hygiene. But it worked against him in the crucial home game against the Netherlands.

This was expected to be our hardest fixture but we played well to go 2-0 up after twenty-four minutes through goals by Barnes and Platt. Although Bergkamp scored a fantastic goal ten minutes later, we were well in control. I was having one of my best games for England and although the Dutch had good players, we felt comfortable against them. Then Gazza was injured. Going up for a header with Jan Wouters, whom he had been winding up the whole evening with his repertoire of insults and gestures. Gazza, of course, never meant anything personal by what he did (it was merely a tactic, a bit of frisky exuberance) but maybe Wouters thought differently. In any case he caught Gazza with an elbow in his face, causing a depressed fracture of the cheekbone. He, Wouters, denies it was intentional but it was still a sending off offence, however he stayed on the field and the Netherlands equalised in the eighty-fifth minute when Des Walker was exposed by Marc Overmars' pace and conceded a penalty. Actually, we thought the foul happened outside the area but a spot-kick was given and Walker was booked.

As I said before, hindsight is a wonderful thing but in point of fact hindsight is often quite a shit thing. Gazza's injury, Wouters not being sent off, a penalty being awarded. All these came back to mock us in a particularly cruel and ironic way a few weeks later during the return match in Rotterdam. At the time, we were just pissed off that we'd outplayed a good team, thrown away a two-goal lead, and come away with only a point. Still, the performance was good and the press, waiting to put the boot in on Taylor, gave him a stay of execution. They even gave me good notices and a few singled me out as man of the match.

Before that, we had away fixtures against Poland (a decent 1-1 draw) and Norway, who were proving to be the surprise team of the group. Attempting to counter Norway's long ball game, Taylor played with three centre backs, which was an unfamiliar system to us. We were also knackered after the Poland game and were battered by the muscular, direct Norwegians. They were better than many gave them credit for but, even so, we should have coped. As Les Ferdinand commented to me afterwards, 'That was particularly shit'. Taylor apologised, the press were after him again ('Norse Manure'), and we found ourselves in the humiliating position of having to win our last three games in the group to qualify for the World Cup in 1994. Even a trip to the States to take part in the U.S. Cup went wrong as we lost the first game 2-0 to the Americans ('Yanks 2 Planks 0'). Despite a good draw against Brazil and playing decently against Germany, Taylor was by then a dead man walking.

Although I didn't see him between games and subsequently wasn't able to feel especially close to him, I had a great deal of sympathy for the man. The press didn't like him and took every opportunity to have a go. He was simply too kind and too open for his own good. Plus he never recovered from having substituted Gary Lineker in the European Championship match against Sweden. He made himself an easy target for journalists who looked for easy, reader-pleasing copy. Neither was he one of them, a southerner, nor, indeed, a characterful archetype from the north. Unfashionably, Taylor was from Scunthorpe ('the cunt out of Scunthorpe' as one of the journalists called him), spent his playing days at dreary Lincoln and boring Grimsby, and wasn't even a goalscoring forward. Later, he managed unfashionable Watford, married a woman called Rita, and at one point lived in Cleethorpes. The press hated his normalcy and seized on every bad result and moment of ill-fortune to vilify him. I had sympathy with him because I was similarly uncool in the eyes of the press. I was merely a working class boy who had fulfilled his potential through hard graft rather than the possession of dazzling skills. Nor did I look the part – a gangling Bambi-on-ice of a player. Perhaps worst of all, cup finals excepted, I never took money from a journalist or offered one a good story. I gave the press nothing and they repaid me with wary indifference and barely supressed scorn occasionally shading into snide disrespect. I wasn't their idea of a football player let alone an England player, and I did little to make life easier for myself. 'Fuck 'em,' I always thought (and sometimes said).

The return match against the Netherlands therefore assumed momentous proportions. Not only was World

Cup qualification hanging on it but I felt that Taylor's career and maybe my own were on the line. Of course, there's always extra pressure playing for your country but my way of dealing with it was to put everything in a box and just focus on the game. Nothing else mattered. Playing for England was a serious matter.

The mood amongst the players leading up to the crucial game against the Netherlands in Rotterdam was pretty buoyant. Remembering the dominant performance of the Wembley game, we were confident we could get a result. In fact, the Dutch needed to win more than we did – they had dropped a point against Norway – and a draw wouldn't have been a bad result for us. But Taylor wanted a win. All the pre-match talk from him was about winning the game. We trained for a win. He knew they would play three pretty static centre backs and felt we could exploit them on the flanks. I'm not sure whether that was a sensible tactic but even if it was, he made a mistake playing me out of position on the right side of midfield. The only reason he did this was because Paul Ince lobbied hard for the central midfield position, arguing that he played there for Manchester United and should therefore do so for his country. Now, no one admires Ince more than I do but I immediately felt put out by this. Ince was equally at home on the right as he was in the middle whereas I was much better suited to a central role. Taylor caved in. As usual, his assistants – Lawrie McMenemy and Phil Neale – said nothing. And I just got on with it.

The Stadion Feijenoord in Rotterdam was a rickety, hostile ground, not really a stadium so much as series of asymmetrical stands crowding the pitch. The atmosphere was aggressive and unfriendly but we were calm, even confident. There was no thought of losing. Ron Atkinson always used to say that before signing a player at Manchester United, he would walk them out to the centre of the pitch at Old Trafford and sneak a look at their eyes. He reckoned he could tell if someone was mentally capable of playing for an iconic club and coping with the pressure of big games just by observing them. I believed him and over the years worked out how to spot players who would fall apart under stress. On my debut for Albion against Newcastle, with 50,000 Geordies calling me all the names under the sun (and some I hadn't heard of), I'd almost come apart, vowing it would never happen again. And after a year or so in the game, I learnt to smell fear in a player and (believe me) not one of the England team that night was afraid, either of the occasion or of losing.

The match has become notorious for two reasons and I had a ringside seat for both of them. First, we lost the match under controversial circumstances. For most of the game, we outplayed the Dutch. It was 0-0 at half-time, though Tony Dorigo hit the post with a fantastic left-foot strike. We went into the dressing room a little disappointed not to be leading but feeling pretty pleased with ourselves. I felt I had done well, albeit in a relatively unfamiliar position, and in addition to my usual defensive duties had played a couple of really good balls into dangerous positions.

I was certainly not expecting to be substituted.

'Carlton, I'm taking you off,' Taylor said as I rested and tried to refocus for the second half.

'Take me off?'

'Yes.'

'Why?'

'Tactical decision.'

'What does that mean?'

'It means I'm putting on Andy Sinton.'

'Andy Sinton?'

'Yes. I think his pace will worry the Dutch. Merson is causing them problems with his speed. They don't like quick players running at them. It's our best chance of winning.'

'But we're doing all right as we are.'

'You and de Boer are just cancelling each other out.'

'Isn't that a good thing?'

'Sorry. It's still our best chance of winning.'

So I sat in the dugout watching the calamity of the second half unfold. Koeman fouled David Platt inside the area and should have conceded a penalty and been sent off. Neither happened. The resulting free kick was charged down by an encroaching Dutchman. Then the Netherlands were awarded a free kick just outside our penalty area and the first attempt was charged down in identical fashion except this time the referee ordered it to be retaken. The second attempt from Koeman, who should not have even been on the pitch, was chipped more or less into the centre of the goal and beyond a badly positioned David Seaman, who had perhaps been unsettled by the retake. Then we hit the post again. And then Bergkamp scored a second goal for the Dutch after first controlling the ball with his hand. Wouters committed a terrible foul for which he ought to have seen an automatic red card, but didn't. Given the circumstances of the Wembley match – the penalty, Gazza's injury, Wouters not being dismissed – it was a horrible way to lose a match we should probably have won. The key moments in the two matches became weird mirror images of each other. Now people say what happened was ironic. It wasn't ironic. It was fucking dreadful. And the referee, Karl

Josef Assenmacher, was piss-poor, in fact he was dropped by FIFA for his next World Cup tie following the debacle.

After the game, Koeman apologised – apparently he apologised to Platt, too, immediately after the foul – and several of the Dutch team said they had got out of jail. In the dressing room, Taylor said that despite the result, our performance was 'outstanding'. I was tempted to say that by substituting me at half-time too much space had been freed up and this had contributed to the way the game had opened up and, unhappily, to the loss.

Mind you, Taylor said a lot of other things on the touchline while the game was slipping away from us. This was the second and secondary drama to which I had a ringside seat. He realised that his job was under threat and made the point to one of the fourth officials, Marcus Merk, saying, 'You see, at the end of the day, I get the sack'. Then he said to one of the linesmen, 'I'm just saying to your colleague, the referee has got me the sack. Thank him ever so much for that, won't you?'

There was something awful about this, I mean apart from having to watch a decent man coming apart. The language Taylor used was somehow both offensive and pusillanimous, the 'thank him ever so much for that' sounding like something your frigging aunt might say. The tap on the linesman's shoulder was both invasive and apologetic. Politely English and rudely un-English at the same time. The whole episode seemed to confirm Taylor as somehow indeterminate, neither one thing nor the other.

For about thirty minutes, he lost his head, almost didn't seem to know who he was, and I listened as he turned the air blue. Earlier, in a match against Poland, also part of the documentary, he had coined a phrase which has since become part of the English language – 'Do I not like that'. Afterwards, Taylor said the swearing was out of character and that he'd used up his annual quota of 'fucks' in one go. Only a handful of people would have heard the foul-mouthed tirade if it hadn't been for the presence of a Channel 4 television crew making a documentary called *An Impossible Job*. I don't know what the fuck the FA was doing in granting them permission to make the programme in the first place. It was bound to end in disaster. To his credit, Taylor said that he was against the programme and hated the idea of having to wear a concealed microphone, but would not 'act' for the cameras. Once again, his honesty in relation to the media and his lack of artifice was the undoing of him.

While I was watching the game and observing Taylor, it also dawned on me that he would lose his job and that very probably his demise would signal the end of my own international career. He was the one who had given me my first cap and in a weird sort of way I was identified as one of his picks, a symbol of his reign. Watching him crumble was in that sense doubly and almost personally painful.

When Taylor resigned after the final, fruitless qualifying game against San Marino, against whom I was a substitute, and Terry Venables was appointed as the new England manager, Ron Atkinson told me I would not be picked. He made the point that Venables understood the media and would most likely make them a sacrificial offering. He was proved correct when I was the only player from the previous squad not named in the new one.

If we'd qualified and Taylor had kept his job, I'm convinced I'd have gone to the World Cup. Do I regret not having that experience? Of course I fucking do! I was proud to represent my country and wanted to be the best player I could be. I was, after all, a working class kid with limited ability who got where he was through hard work and an ability to read the game. Perhaps eighteen caps was my allotted number. And if someone had told me when I was a boy that I would play for England just once then I'd have settled for that. All the same, I honestly felt that I was a better defender than, for example, Gareth Southgate, who went on to win a load of caps – but there was no bitterness from me. It is what it is and I moved on. I don't dwell on things and, my divorce apart, I rarely linger. Besides, Paul Scholes was just around the corner for England, so how bad was that? Although I knew my international career was over after the Dutch game, and I never did play again for my country, the day after returning from Rotterdam, on 14th October, my daughter Kelly was born. I was there for the birth. Life striking back! And on the Saturday, we played Sheffield United in the Sheffield derby.

10

The Pricks

'I am Jesus whom thou persecutest: it is hard for thee to kick against the pricks.' Acts of the Apostles, chapter 9, verse 5

I'm just off the phone to my daughter, Nicole. She's called me because she's had an argument with Jenny, her mum. I've had a long day at work, running the Academy at Wellington College in Shanghai. My legs ache because I've also been taking fitness classes, mostly with mums who want to work out, keep their figures, get their figures back, or in some cases get figures they never had. I arrive at around 7.30 in the morning and get back at close to 8.30 in the evening. I like my work, I like my days, so I can't complain. But I'm knackered. Lucy has cooked me a meal and I don't really want to think about much except a glass of red wine, maybe watching a film on DVD, and getting some sleep. Due to the time difference – we are eight hours ahead in China – it is not unreasonable for Nicole to call me at this time. I listen and try to understand what's gone on, then talk to her about what has happened, telling her that she must find a way of working through the problem. As I have spent much of my own life working through problems, including working through problems with Nicole and my other two kids, Kelly and Jordan, I feel as if I am reasonably well qualified to talk to my own daughter about working through problems.

When I have finished, Lucy says to me, not unkindly, 'You're forever lecturing your kids, Carlton.'

'I wasn't lecturing. I was giving advice.'

'You were lecturing.'

'It might have sounded like lecturing to you. I was just giving her the benefit of my infinite wisdom.'

'I.e., lecturing.'

'Whatever.'

Lucy has her own daughter, Amy, from a previous marriage. And I have three kids. When we met each other and then got together we talked about having children. It was feasible – just. But there were so many things against it, too, not least the difficult circumstances of my own split from Jenny and the ensuing strains with Kelly, Nicole and Jordan. Lucy and I were very careful not to introduce Amy to my children until we'd been together for a year or so. None of the four children has known anyone other than their own mothers and fathers, plus Lucy and me. To introduce a third element into this very modern family set-up might have caused even more complications. On the other hand, it might have acted as some kind of bond, bringing us even closer together. But it would have been a high-risk strategy, and so arduous had been the process of leaving Jenny that we decided to stick, not twist.

Kelly was born on 14th October 1993. A Sheffield Wednesday baby. Nicole was born on 23rd January 1996. A Leeds United baby. Jordan, who was born on 26th May 1998, would be a Southampton baby. So by the time I joined Leeds United in June 1994 for £2.6 million, I was a

My parents, Linda and Lloyd. This was taken
when they were on a cruise I'd booked for them

With my sisters Sharon (left) and Julie. We had this
photograph taken as part of a Christmas present
for mum and dad

Playing here for West Brom and taking on Everton's Ian Snodin in the FA Cup third round in 1989. I had plenty of battles with 'Snods' throughout my playing career

© Bob Thomas/Getty Images

At Sheffield Wednesday celebrating with Danny Wilson, Roland Nilsson, physio Alan Smith and Viv Anderson after we had beaten Bristol City to gain promotion back to the top division

© Steve Ellis

Against QPR in 1991. I surprisingly scored a hat trick in this game as we gained a 4-1 victory
© *Steve Ellis*

Alongside Martin Keown, Paul Merson, Trevor Steven, David Platt and Gary Lineker for England against Denmark in our first Euro 92 match
© *Chris Smith/ Popperfoto/Getty Images*

With Chris Woods, Paul Gascoigne, David Platt, John Barnes and Nigel Clough in six-a-side training session with the England team at Bisham Abbey. We had just won, hence the pose
© *Steve Morton/Allsport*

Before the FA Cup Final in May 1993. The Duchess of Kent asked me if I was joining Aston Villa, I said I didn't know
© *Steve Ellis*

Now at Leeds United and getting my name on the scoresheet again
© *Andrew Varley*

Manchester United always gave us a hard battle and Paul Ince was a superb box-to-box midfielder
© *Andrew Varley*

At The Dell with Southampton in 1998 and there was only ever going to be one winner for the ball. Newcastle's Nikolaos Dabizas never stood a chance
© *Phil Cole/Allsport*

Back at Elland Road with Nottingham Forest in 1999 and this was never a red card! My pal Lucas Radebe argues my case
© *Andrew Varley*

Playing for Coventry in 1999. Marcus Hall, Gary McAllister and Youssef Chippo look on as I tackle Aston Villa's Julian Joachim and win the ball
© *Ben Radford/Allsport*

In my role as player/ manager with Stockport County in 2001 as we take on Burnley at Turf Moor. Kevin Richardson, Colin Murphy the doctor and Craig Madden are alongside me
© Alex Livesey/Allsport

With Seth Johnson and Lee Hendrie at the dinner after an England v Scotland Veterans game in Dubai

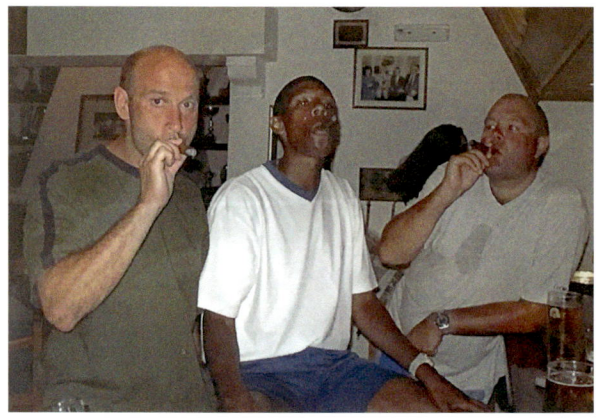

Before my wedding to Lucy. My best man Greg Towers is on my left and my good friend Nigel Gilbert is on my right

Getting married to Lucy in June 2007 was one of
the happiest days of my life

© James Stewart

Our wedding at Hassop Hall in Derbyshire. I'm with Lucy, her sister, my
best man Greg, nephew and nieces and our children

© James Stewart

Lucy's fortieth birthday fancy dress party

Relaxing with a beer on holiday in Thailand

Left to right, my children Jordan, Kelly and Nicole

father and, within eighteen months, the family would have doubled in number.

I'd always wanted a family. This comes from my mum, I think, who always stressed the importance of flesh and blood, of kin. And I inherited her old-fashioned views about family, immediately feeling the pull of responsibility, the need to protect, the obligation to provide.

In part, all this was an influence on the move to Leeds. I'd all but signed for Ron at Aston Villa when Leeds came in with a bid. Although the financial package on offer at Elland Road was good – I would suddenly find myself earning serious money – I had also put down roots in Yorkshire and was in the process of renovating a house. Or, more accurately, creating a home for my family. Leeds still trained at Elland Road (before they moved to a new training facility) and I could get to the ground in a little over thirty minutes.

Like so many decisions, you go with a gut feeling and then construct reasons to justify what is usually an emotional choice. I also liked Howard Wilkinson, another kind of father figure, a schoolmasterly one, which isn't that surprising seeing that he used to be a teacher before he became a football manager. He talked of playing me in the middle of the defence and of this being the key to me winning back my place in the England team. He was also a very honourable bloke and, contrary to the popular image of him, a humane and wry man with a subtle sense of humour. When we were working through my contract, he said that if I played well and did the business for him then I would never have to seek him out: 'I will come to you.' And this is exactly what he did after I'd been at the club for eighteen months. He called me into his office, ripped up my contract, and offered me improved terms. A man of his word.

Mind you, the words we had weren't always so agreeable. Another time, he invited me into his office and asked me sit down. Whenever he asked someone to sit down you knew there was an issue.

'Carlton … I've got something to ask you.'

'Yes, boss.'

'I don't want you to take this the wrong way.'

'I'll try not to take it the wrong way.'

'It's about drinking.'

'Yes.'

'Your drinking.'

'Yes.'

'Have you ever thought about *not* drinking?'

'Not really.'

'Maybe it's something to think about.'

'In what way?'

'In the way that you should think about not drinking.'

'Why should I think about not drinking?'

And then he gave me a list, not quite in alphabetical order, but nevertheless substantial. It included things like playing better, regaining my England place, and prolonging my career. As he was talking to a recently self-proclaimed family man with obligations, financial and otherwise, he pressed all the right buttons. I was willing to consider anything he might say that would enhance my life as a professional footballer. So I gave it a go. I, Carlton Palmer, tried to abstain from alcohol.

It was around this time that Tony Adams, who I knew from England games, admitted to problems with alcoholism. And Arsene Wenger was about to be appointed manager at Arsenal, somehow acting as a focal point and articulating what people were anyway beginning to say about the effect of diet and drinking on players. So I thought, yeah, fuck it: why not?

Me being me, I went pell-mell at abstinence. I gave it up altogether and embraced a regime of sobriety. I dried out hard. I trained hard. If anything, and if it were possible, even harder than before. I turned not drinking into a crusade and didn't drink *at all*.

And guess what? I started to play shit. The more I didn't drink, the worse I played. At first, I was dimly aware that my performances weren't up to scratch. Then, when things didn't get any better, I started to fret about the way I played the game and even about my standing as professional footballer.

Wilkinson dropped me for a game against Manchester United, the first time in my life this had happened, and I found myself playing in a reserve team match.

He called me into his office again.

'Sit down, Carlton.'

I sat down. Sullen.

'I'm sorry about this, Carlton. But you're not playing well.'

'I know.'

'What's going on?'

'I don't know. I'm training hard. Everything is going fine … except on match days …'

'Anything different?'

'How do you mean?'

'Are you doing anything different than you were before?'

'Just the one thing.'

'What's that?'

'The obvious one …'

'Yes …'

'I'm not drinking.'

'Are you sure?'

'Not a drop. Not one single fucking drop.'

'You're certain about that?'

'Yeah. Trust me. I've stopped altogether.'

He thought about this for a moment, then got out of his seat, went to the fridge in his office, opened it, pulled out a can of lager, handed it to me, and said, 'There you go, Carlton. See if that helps.'

So I started drinking again, after which my performances improved and normal service was resumed.

I've considered this. Clearly it's not a blueprint that most sportsmen should adopt. But in my particular case maybe there's a *need* for drink. Maybe there's a simple physiological need for the sugar? Or maybe – and this feels more likely – I need the drink as something to kick against, something against which I can push and strive. A kind of internal mechanism that enables me to find another gear. This is difficult to explain and even harder to justify. However, I do know that when I go to the gym the morning after a heavy drinking session, I often record my best times on the treadmill. And Paul Walsh once told me, after we'd been out drinking the night before a game in which he wasn't actually playing, that he was astonished I could play the way I did after such conspicuous consumption. As I've already described, this isn't always what happens, but in my case, there is evidence to suggest that drinking provides me with a psychological edge I would otherwise not possess. I need pricks to kick against, and booze is my prick.

***

Playing for Sheffield Wednesday was like being in a family. Playing at Leeds was like joining a business, getting a job. The expectations were greater. The club believed it could win things (it had recently won the old First Division title). The fans expected to win things (many of them could remember the glory days, twenty years ago, when Leeds was the most powerful team in the country). The club and the fans presumed they had a right to success. At Wednesday, we were encouraged to entertain and to express ourselves. At Leeds, the talk was of not losing more than three games in the season if we wanted to win the league. A defeat, any defeat, was the prelude to a bout of soul-searching and a damning statistic to be weighed up, considered, the reasons for it discovered, and culprits unearthed.

Wilkinson was structured and had plans for each game. For him, everything was thought-out and meticulous. I liked that about him, as I liked his assertiveness and matter-of-fact manner, the authoritativeness coated by a dry, witty humanity. I learnt that Gordon Strachan had been instrumental in bringing me to Leeds. He was a fantastic footballer in a team of gifted, hard professionals that included Gary Speed, David O'Leary and Gary McAllister. We should have won things; as it turned out, we won nowt. The nearest we came was a League Cup Final against Aston Villa where for some reason we were flat and played like shit. Villa won 3-0. They were worthy winners. I knew that Ron, who was managing them, would have found a way of relaxing them before the game and that's exactly what happened – they played with a sense of calm, loose self-belief whereas we froze.

Leeds was the first club I played for where I felt that I was going into work every day and doing a job. This didn't mean that I didn't enjoy it and it's not necessarily a criticism – and, of course, I was well-paid for the privilege – but suddenly things felt different.

On a pre-season tour to Malaysia, we all turned up at the airport in club blazers and travelled Business Class. This was a different kind of operation to the ones I'd been used to. Wilkinson was in the seat immediately in front of me, immaculate and pristine, looking the business and through looking the business *being* the business. I asked one of the cabin crew for a drink. David O'Leary, who was sitting next to me, said drinking whilst travelling on club business was not allowed. I liked David but there was also something unctuous about him, as if locating the party line and then holding to it was a little bit too important. So I leant forward to Wilkinson, and said, 'Would it be ok if I ordered a drink?' 'No problem,' he said. One or two of the others complained and said it had never been allowed before. 'You've never asked me before,' said Wilkinson, with a paternal glint.

Later, Gary McAllister and I argued about something, I can't recall what, the drink having loosened our tongues. We got off on the wrong foot, the argument merely being a pretext for the coming together of two egos. We were very different players and were both pretty full of ourselves. Although our playing styles should have complemented each other, and this was the reason why we'd been brought together at Leeds, there was also tension between us.

This came to a head in a game against Ipswich in November 1994 when we lost 2-0 to a team we should have comfortably beaten and were themselves relegated at the end of the season. The first Ipswich goal involved a simple ball over the top of our defence and into the path of the eventual scorer – who should have been tracked by Gary.

Instead, he merely trotted behind the runner, never getting close enough to prevent the ball arriving or getting in a tackle, then forlornly raising an arm to appeal for offside as the ball was steered into the net.

As we came off at half-time, I launched into Gary, bollocking him for what I said was 'standing-still football'.

'That was fucking disgraceful,' I said.

'Fuck off,' Gary replied.

'You're supposed to track runners, not fucking wave them through.'

'Still fuck off.'

'You didn't even get a tackle in. Fucking pathetic.'

And it continued into the dressing room, if anything increasing in intensity.

When Wilkinson came in, McAllister said, 'Are you going to let him talk to me like that?' Clearly he felt I was undermining his status as a senior professional. I can't remember what Wilkinson said, if anything, but whatever it was, Gary clearly felt he wasn't being supported or supported enough. Our relationship at Leeds was therefore awkward, which isn't to say that McAllister wasn't a great footballer (he was), or lazy (he certainly was not), or that we didn't make up and become friends (we did, eventually).

Wilkinson's response to this was to involve us both in decision-making, a sensitive and intelligent way to bring together two clashing egos. To that extent, it worked, and whilst we played together there was never much of a problem on the pitch. But it was only later, when Gary and I were both at Coventry, that we actually became friends.

Although I enjoyed my time at Leeds, I was beginning to realise how exceptional my time at Wednesday had been. Maybe my time at Leeds coincided with the way the game was changing, from a game to a business, the economic consequences of forming the Premier League in 1992 now beginning to bite in terms of its culture, the feel and texture of football itself.

Whatever the reasons, I remember reflecting that although I was employed in a lucrative and specialised industry, that was – give or take – what it now was: an industry. And I was an 'employee', a hired hand. The notion of becoming a strolling mercenary had never occurred to me before, but the league was suddenly employing overseas players, not merely because they were good but also because they were generally cheaper than their British counterparts.

Jenny and I had started a family, and I'm pretty convinced this was related to my life as a footballer. I was on something of a treadmill, the football becoming an occupation, a profession, and the marriage becoming one of familial duty. In their own ways, both were lines of work, which isn't to say that they weren't enjoyable. They were. And I loved having kids. But I'm also aware, looking back, that divorce was never far away. It was only once I'd stopped playing football that marriage to Jenny began to come into some kind of realistic focus. Everything was a means to an end: the football begat money; the money begat security; the security begat a family.

These things were symbolised by the building of a house, a family home, 'The Hawthorns', oddly enough next door to Howard Wilkinson's place. My mum described it as being 'like something out of *Dallas*', and I suppose it was. The original building was ripped apart on the inside so that renovations could take place and things like a bar (including Guinness on tap), a snooker room, bespoke bedrooms, a kids' playroom, and a cinema were built. It was set in several acres of its own grounds. Italian marble with the words 'The Hawthorns' inscribed on it was ordered for the front gate, this – ironically – arriving on the day that Jenny and I separated and moved out of the house.

But for the moment, there was a rhythm, a pattern, a tempo to my life in which everything seemed financially and professionally connected. Not so much *Roy of the Rovers* as *Carlton the careful.* I was getting on with life. I was getting things done.

In my three years at Leeds, we reached a cup final, had a brief and inglorious run in Europe, finished 5th in the Premier League during my first season, and then hovered in mid-table for the others. This wasn't the kind of return Leeds was banking on and Wilkinson was sacked. He was followed by George Graham, who had previously been manager at Arsenal and had just finished serving a one-year suspension from the game for taking illegal payments from an agent.

Almost immediately, I didn't like him. He arrived at Elland Road carrying an Arsenal bag. He seemed intent on picking on all the high wage earners in the club, one of whom was me, presumably with the intention of making examples of the senior professionals and thereby gaining control of the dressing room. He was a swaggering bully of a man, his debonair appearance never quite able to obscure the jutting, single-minded chin and resolute, unbending jaw. In many ways, he was a throw-back, a disciplinarian whose methods were unsuited to the developing world of football that accommodated highly paid players who didn't have to take the kind of shit people like Graham were used to dishing out. Leeds was his last hurrah, and in that sense he was emblematic of a dying breed, the old sports teacher who thought naughty children could be made better by making them do ten press-ups. Ian Rush advised me to suck it up and lie low but I couldn't hide my distaste for the manager and his methods.

Pretty soon, he took the club captaincy off me. That cost me two thousand quid per game. Then he made it clear that he wanted me out, though he forbade me joining all Premier League clubs other than Southampton, who looked like they were nailed on for relegation. 'It's the south coast or the Championship for you, son,' was the way he put it. The only good thing about Graham was that he jolted me out of my passive acceptance of the way my life was going. He became the latest and biggest prick I was kicking against.

11

Talk is Cheap

'I do reinvent old hits of mine and sort of give them a new life.'
Christina Aguilera

There are political talks going on in Beijing at the moment. Normally this would not be something that would hold any interest for me or to which I would pay much attention. However, for their duration, the Chinese authorities have turned off or blocked almost all the VPNs in the country. A VPN is a Virtual Private Network, which allows people to open their computers and override public networks, which are frequently censored in China. When your VPN is inhibited, the average Brit living in China is hit hard. No Facebook, for example. Or Google. Or YouTube.

It's early March and the weather in Shanghai is turning from winter to spring, or more likely from winter to summer. One day it is cold and bleak, the next it is sunny and bright. Although there are seasons here, the transition between them is abrupt. The end of winter arrives as if an axe had been taken to it. The only evidence of spring is a temporary crispness in the air and the evidence of pollen, which requires warnings on our mobile phones and, for many, the donning of a mask. I don't wear a mask. I look like a twat in a mask. Lucy and I have talked about it on several occasions but the bottom line – or at least my bottom line – is that a mask will make me look like something out of a horror film. Many of the Chinese wear masks but their faces – dainty, elflike, fine-featured – can carry it off. Today, though, the pollen in the air is tangible: microscopic, powdery grains barrel down Huaihai Road, whipped up by a strong wind, stinging people's eyes, causing them to protect their faces, shield their eyes, and turn away from the pall of dust.

I am watching all this from the apartment, high up on the twenty-first floor. Pissed off by the lack of entertainment available to me on my laptop, the only things I have been able to discover, by looking at the *The Guardian* website, is that the showing of gay romance has been officially banned from Chinese television and that Tony Warren, the gay creator of *Coronation Street*, has died. If I could be bothered to think about it, I suspect these two facts would illuminate something significant about one of the differences between life in China and life in the UK.

Lucy suggests I try listening to Talksport, which in the past has escaped the VPN clampdown. And she's right. It has. When I manage to connect, I arrive in the middle of an interview with Matt Le Tissier, with whom I used to play after leaving Leeds to go to Southampton. Le Tissier answers a question about the lack of success for the English football team by saying that it's because we pick players 'like Carlton Palmer'.

'I can't believe he's said that,' I called out to Lucy.

'What's that?' she yelled back, doing something in another room.

'Fucking Le Tissier. He's had another fucking pop at me.'

And, indeed, fucking Le Tissier had had a previous fucking pop at me. This was in his autobiography, in which he spent pretty much a whole chapter saying that I was a bully. At the time, what he said disappointed me. But I more or less let it go. Let him say what he wants. If he feels the need to make a few more quid by distorting the truth, that's his business.

But this latest barb, unwarranted and cheap, pissed me off. The subtext, of course, is that England didn't pick players like Matt Le Tissier. The subtext is that Matt Le Tissier is a sublimely gifted footballer who wasn't given enough chances by his national team to prove his worth. The subtext is that if players like Matt Le Tissier and, of course and in particular, Matt Le Tissier himself, had been picked more often, then England would have done better. The subtext is that England persists in picking players who aren't as good or as skillful or as talented as Matt Le Tissier. The subtext is that Carlton Palmer represents all those players who aren't as good or as skillful or as talented as Matt Le Tissier. The subtext is that Carlton Palmer is an easy target because regardless of the facts, Carlton Palmer does not look like a footballer or play the game in the way that many football fans imagine it should be played. The subtext is that Matt Le Tissier represents all the wasted opportunities that England has had in picking the 'right' players and that Carlton Palmer represents all the ill-advised choices it actually made. The subtext is that I, Matt Le Tissier, am a much better player than he, Carlton Palmer, and that it's just *not fair* that he played eighteen times (one goal) for England and I only played eight times (no goals).

I have already mentioned the fact that I have become an easy victim of the game people play in naming their worst England sides. I wouldn't say it's yet become a cliché, though there's little doubt that it's a comment that can be made without too much fear of contradiction and that it plays to an uncomplicated, gullible, guffawing audience.

And, of course, Le Tissier has a yen for recognition and acceptance. He has an easy-going, amiable, jokey persona, which is wheeled out on television, his well-upholstered body, snaggle-toothed grin, and boy-next-door mop of hair allowing him a non-threatening, cosy, almost neighbourly demeanour. Everyone loves Matt Le Tissier, so when he says something apparently funny and deliberately hurtful about Carlton Palmer there's a fair chance that people will go along with it. It's a line that keeps on giving.

When I first arrived at Southampton, the kit man had put my kit out and I began to change. Le Tissier arrived a few minutes later and told me to move, saying that he'd 'always' changed there. It was his place.

'Well, you aren't getting changed here today,' I said.

'You what?' he replied.

'You aren't getting changed here today,' I repeated. 'I am.'

If he'd asked me nicely, I like to think I'd have moved. Generally, I don't give a flying fuck where I change. Or rather, I'd just arrived at the club and didn't give a flying fuck at that particular moment. But he made it into a *thing*. He challenged me and I rarely back down in those situations.

It soon became pretty clear to me that Le Tissier thought he had a special place at the club.

Apart from that, I don't recall ever having a confrontation with him or anyone else at Southampton apart from, occasionally, on the field. But he was used to getting his own way, the fans loved him, and he was very comfortable there.

The other thing that soon became pretty clear to me was that Le Tissier wasn't fit. More than that, he didn't want to do the work that would enable him to get fit and make him a better player. It even got to the point where I thought he should not be picked for the team. When I voiced this opinion to the manager, Dave Jones, he said, 'If I don't play him, I'll get the sack'.

Having said that, there was never any doubt that Le Tissier was a very gifted player. He had two good feet, terrific skill, and was an excellent finisher. He scored a lot of goals for Southampton. Mind you, he also took all the penalties and free kicks, so there were plenty of opportunities. But despite this and the folk hero status he acquired at the club, for someone of such talent there was also a sense of having squandered a gift.

For various reasons, he was just too content and cosy at Southampton. And I reckon some of it was to do with a lack of ambition. Simple as. I know that a number of the big clubs looked at him and wanted to take him, but Le Tissier never seemed to want to challenge himself and improve himself as a professional footballer. The 'one club player' tag looks endearing from the outside and nourishes fans' views of him as a loyal and principled man – I understand that – but the reality was different. He just couldn't be arsed. The reality was: Matt Le Tissier – plenty of talent and no hard work: eight England caps; Carlton Palmer – not so talented and plenty of hard work: eighteen England caps. It pissed him off. It would have pissed me off. The difference is, I'd have done something about it.

Glenn Hoddle and Terry Venables were the England

managers who picked Le Tissier for their teams, yet neither felt confident enough to give him an extended run in the side. Venables had made me something of a scapegoat for the failure to qualify for the 1994 World Cup in the USA, and you would have thought that selecting Le Tissier might have been a tempting call for him to make, a statement of intent, as it were. You know, a declaration of his plans to make England a stylish and entertaining side. But it never really happened. And you would have thought, also, that Glenn Hoddle, himself an elegant and naturally gifted player, much like Le Tissier, would have been drawn to him. But that never really happened, either. He was left out of the squad for the 1998 World Cup in France, something which still wrankles with him. In effect, Le Tissier knows he pissed away a prodigious talent.

Hoddle was an aloof and rather awkward man, but he understood that in addition to being able to kick a football, players also had to work hard. And Hoddle himself, despite the media's typecasting of him as a nimble-footed show-pony, always put in a good shift.

Actually, and gradually after the initial problems about whereabouts in the dressing room we should be changing, Le Tissier and I became – or I thought we had become – reasonably friendly. Understanding that we were more or less stuck with each other, a system was devised whereby three midfield players who had energy, mobility and pace (myself, Matt Oakley and Kevin Richardson) did all the fetching and carrying, thus creating the space in which Le Tissier could operate. Dave Jones knew that he couldn't select his most naturally gifted player either in midfield or as an out-and-out striker, but as something in-between, with space and time served up to him on plate. I assumed that bridges had been built with Le Tissier. After a difficult start, he gravitated towards the group of players who minded him whilst he was playing and gave him the license to do more or less as he pleased. We spent time together. There was even some kind of camaraderie between us.

And I was enjoying my time at Southampton. The bad taste of my departure from Leeds – 'You're a good player but you're not going anywhere where you might embarrass me,' George Graham had said – was washed away by my stay on the south coast.

I liked Dave Jones, a calm and intelligent man who understood why teams needed both a Le Tissier and a Palmer in their sides. He tolerated my occasional excesses explaining that he knew I worked hard and would always do the business when and where it mattered. I liked the players, too. Paul Jones, Jason Dodd, Ken Monkou, Francis Benali, John Beresford … all good professionals and decent blokes.

In a strange way, I also liked the relative lack of expectation. Finishing mid-table for Southampton was fine. All the same, when I arrived, the club was anchored to the bottom of the Premier League. They were the only club in the top division that Graham would make it easy for me to join. I wanted a clause put into my contract that I would receive a £75,000 bonus if we got into Europe.

Rupert Lowe, the chairman, said, 'You're taking the piss'.

I said, 'How am I taking the piss?'

'Because we're bottom of the league. All we want to do is avoid relegation.'

'Well, if I'm taking the piss and getting into Europe is so impossible then there won't be a problem about putting it into the contract, will there?'

In the end, we surged up the table and by Christmas, despite being adrift at the bottom after six or seven games, most bookmakers had stopped accepting bets on us being relegated. Despite there being an outside chance of European football, our form fell away in the final weeks of the season and we settled for twelfth place. All the players apart from me were on a bonus merely for staying in the division; once this was assured, our performances lost the edge that had taken us up the table.

All the same, I felt a new sense of life. I liked Southampton and I loved playing football again after the complications at Leeds. I was on a lower salary but this didn't matter. I just wanted to play, and the high-energy, unafraid, unencumbered style of play at The Dell suited me very well, as did the small pitch and its close proximity to the noisy, passionate supporters.

Two or three months after joining, I scored a spectacular goal against Sheffield Wednesday, swinging my foot through a rising ball on the edge of the penalty area, the shot spearing across the 'keeper and thumping into the back of the net from an acute angle. You have to see this in context. I don't usually score goals and I certainly don't usually score goals like that. But the moment seemed to sum up what I was feeling during my time at the club: don't be afraid, try something, *have a go*. Even fucking Le Tissier would have been proud of it.

***

We'd just finished a game and had to be in for training on Tuesday. Like me, David Hirst, with whom I'd played at

Wednesday, still had a home in Sheffield. He didn't fancy the drive back north. Neither did I, if the truth be told. Jenny and I were still together but it was very much a routine, a habit, even a chore. A marriage by numbers.

'Let's do something,' he said.

'What?'

He thought for a minute. 'Cheltenham. Let's go to Cheltenham for the festival.'

So we made a plan to go and watch the horseracing, though we were immediately discouraged by the traffic reports and the length of time it would take to get there.

So overnight we booked a helicopter to pick us up after Tuesday training. Then, on Monday evening, he called a friend who owned a gentleman's outfitters, and we got fixed up with morning suits to wear in the owners' enclosure.

The next day, as the Tuesday training session drew to a close, Dave Jones came marching across the pitch. 'Is anyone here taking the piss?' he shouted at the squad. We all looked at him with blank expressions. One or two of the players, who knew what was happening, tried to hide their smirks. 'I said, is anyone here taking the fucking piss?' Jones repeated.

'What's the problem?' someone asked.

'I've just had fucking air traffic control on the phone requesting permission for a fucking helicopter to land.'

Then, from a mile or so away, faint at first and increasingly discernible, came the unmistakable juddering noise of helicopter blades slicing through the air. Everyone looked up. A small helicopter hovered into view, bucking slightly in the blustery spring wind, before setting down in the middle of the pitch and then settling itself there like a sleepy cat about to take a nap.

Hirst and I had arranged for a car to bring our suits to the session at the appropriate time, and this now duly arrived. As the helicopter came to a standstill, we grabbed the suits from the car, each donning a pair of sunglasses as we did so, ran over to the chopper, and then, still in our sweaty kit, climbed aboard. As we rose into the air, waving to all the players, I could see Dave Jones shouting, 'Fuck off!' though in the nicest way possible.

Hirst and I spent the day in the bar at Cheltenham with Alan McInally. I don't think we saw any horseracing. On our return to Southampton, Dave Jones didn't mention it. I was enjoying life again.

***

I was playing well because I was happy and I was happy because I was playing well. Southampton was like a new start. I even had a new girlfriend, Simone, who I had met in a nightclub almost as soon as I'd arrived on the south coast. Although I wasn't thinking about moving in with Simone, or at least not leaving Jenny because of her, I was aware that my marriage, for all its pragmatism and the sense that our two daughters needed some kind of stability, was a businesslike fiction. In effect, Jenny and I were living separate existences. We were getting on with our lives in matter-of-fact ways, delighted by our children but otherwise disconnected. We weren't yet embittered or angry, merely numb, albeit in a pleasant and affluent way.

Then, everything changed.

Jenny phoned.

'Carlton, I've got something to tell you.'

'Sounds ominous.'

'It is.'
'What's wrong?'
'Nothing's wrong.'
'What then?'
'I'm pregnant.'
'Fucking hell, Jenny.'

I felt torn. On the one hand, I was delighted at the prospect of becoming a dad again. On the other, I had begun to feel that my life had steadied itself and I was enjoying things again, both professionally and, to an extent, personally. Being at Southampton had brought a smile back to my face and had enabled me to balance my work and my domestic life, to take pleasure in the one and to consider alternative arrangements in the other. Jenny's news changed everything.

12

Trouble and Strife

'A good marriage would be between a blind wife and a deaf husband.' Michel de Montaigne

There is a perception amongst the public that footballers not only have the pick of any girl they want but that they also make the most of this situation, i.e. that they spend much of their free time – of which there is generally a great deal – shagging. This is both true and not true at the same time. While it might be an accurate description for some footballers, for others it is not. For every professional footballer who spends much of his career installed in hotel suites with a bevy of willing beauties, there is one who abstains and goes home to the wife and another who occasionally gives in to temptation but is generally well-behaved. Probably, for most of this time, I put myself in the latter category.

Over the years, I have witnessed all kinds of infidelity, though I have never taken an especially judgmental position. High-profile players with loving families who habitually spend time away from their loved ones in bed with a conveyer belt of allocated women; players who lead two existences, double lives that might be discreet or open; players who spend their nights on the phone to their wives and kids, homesick, terrified to venture out of a hotel room lest they fall prey to an attractive groupie; players who bed girls simply because they think it is expected of them and believe it might even help their standing in the group. Neither are managers exempt, though gaffers tend to be more secretive and their extra-marital affairs are more discreet.

Professional football is teeming with temptation, sexual allure, seduction, and urge. Players deal with it in different ways. The modern way is for sex to be forbidden, not from a moral standpoint but because it might have a negative impact on a player's on-field performance and because clubs can do without the headache of intrusive and generally damaging publicity.

But there's no doubt that playing the game at a high level for a number of years brings unwelcome baggage causing suspicion and a lack of trust between couples. One player I know, a lovely man in all other respects (and famous with it), destroyed his wife through his incessant philandering, which was almost institutionalised when he was away from home.

Although I'm very happy with Lucy and our life in Shanghai, I have felt the need to back up my protestations of commitment and affection with material obligation. Pension plans, houses, and investments have all been put in Lucy's name. Everything I own and all my assets are, so far as the law goes, hers. If I stray, she has the wherewithal to clean me out. I should say that Lucy herself neither instigated nor encouraged this arrangement. It is purely of my own devising because I want her to understand how much she means to me. Simple as.

Who knows why I have insisted on this deal? Part of it, I'm sure, is because there are assumptions about professional footballers – they are a group of randy, oversexed, unprincipled men who are incapable of living in a monogamous relationship – that make it difficult to convince a partner that she is 'the one'. To put it another way, why would a woman commit to a man whose history is one of flirtatious philandering?

Only a few weeks ago, I was called in by my current employer and asked about an incident that happened almost twenty years ago. Someone – I have my suspicions who as she has tried this trick before – tipped her off about a conviction for indecent assault. If you Google the incident, you come up with the following baldly-stated facts: 'Soccer star Carlton Palmer was found guilty of groping a teenage girl. Married Palmer, 31, was fined £600 for indecent assault. The ex-England player put his hand between the 18-year-old girl's legs while out drinking with his Leeds United team-mates. Stipendiary magistrate David Loy told him: "I'm conscious of the pressure you've been under as a result of this allegation. I'm also conscious of the effect the conviction will have upon you. As far as the assault was concerned, it was not persistent over a long period nor was it of the gravest nature. But it was a very unpleasant incident indeed." Last week during his trial, Palmer denied the assault. He also said that the charge had put a strain on his marriage and career, costing him the club captaincy. A Leeds court heard that the girl had gone to talk to him and other footballers in the Square on the Lane bar in the city in January. She said Palmer made obscene comments about the size of his manhood before assaulting her. The girl told Palmer that he was out of order and slapped him then complained to a doorman and the police. Palmer and team-mate Lee Sharpe, who gave evidence at the trial, said the girl had persistently tried to find out which nightclub they were going to. Palmer said he swore at the girl and pushed her twice because she would not leave him alone.'

On the face of it, this looks terrible – drunken, arrogant footballer takes advantage of his celebrity status and lewdly attacks young, naïve girl. There's just about enough in the press report to identify a different, less damning, more truthful picture, but the buzzwords are still there: SOCCER STAR, GROPING, TEENAGE GIRL, INDECENT ASSAULT, DRINKING, BAR, OBSCENE, UNPLEASANT INCIDENT. Why wouldn't an employer be worried (though almost twenty years on is perhaps a bit much)? And more to the point, what woman wouldn't be uneasy about committing her life to a man who apparently liked nothing better of an evening than to get drunk, boast about the size of his cock, and stick his hand between a young girl's legs?

I was probably a late starter with girls. I didn't lose my virginity until I was nineteen, which in late twentieth-century England was like not knowing how to ride a bike or open a packet of crisps. There were two reasons for this. My family life was close-knit and old-fashioned in the sense that girls, and especially messing around with girls, was considered unimportant in comparison with things like hard work and making the most of your life. In particular, my dad instilled traditional, Christian values in us. And the second reason was football, about which I was fanatical. Playing, training and thinking about football occupied almost all my waking hours; there wasn't room for anything else.

When I was seventeen or eighteen, I signed as a

professional for West Bromwich Albion, my local club and the one I supported as a boy. All I ever wanted to do was play for them. The manager then was Johnny Giles and the players included people like Cyrille Regis and Derek Statham. I made my debut away at Newcastle in September 1985, only because Jimmy Nicholl was injured. I played at right back but wasn't convincing and didn't become a regular first-team player until a game against Birmingham a few weeks later. It was my home debut and the Man of the Match trophy I won is still on show in my parents' home.

At that time, I was still catching two buses to the ground, one to West Bromwich and another to the Hawthorns. The same again for the return journey. I used to hide at the back of the bus, lying down on the seats so no one would recognise me. Although my life had changed – I was getting £500 a week, more than double what my dad was getting for driving buses – women, drink, and cars were not part of the plan. And remember, my dad told me to buy a house with the money I was getting and even though buying a house was the last thing I wanted to do (what normal nineteen-year old wants to buy a fucking house?), of course, as I've already said, I took his advice and bought a house.

It was probably the best advice anyone has ever given me even if I didn't realise it at the time.

So there I was, a physically imposing nineteen-year old, fit as a fiddle, energy to burn, no doubt awash with spunk, with more money than I knew what to do with, and I spent my time hiding at the back of buses and sleeping. Saturday nights were for lounging in front of the television with a bottle of lager watching *Match of the Day*. I was a shy lad and didn't mix with the Albion first team even though I was theoretically on some kind of par with them. My place wasn't so far from mum and dad's house. It wasn't uncommon for the electric meter to run out midway through the evening, causing me to walk round, borrow some cash, usually 50 pence, and head back to finish the evening's viewing. Probably I wanted to stay. My dad would always tease me about not being able to stay away from home and standing on my own two feet though of course he always made me welcome.

The nearest I came to having a girlfriend was traipsing round a nightclub in Birmingham carrying a girl's coat. I didn't want to be there and had only gone because it was a new club and Albion had asked me and a few others go along to 'represent' them. She was a model for *Ebony* and took full advantage of my naïvety by treating me like some kind of manservant.

Soon afterwards, I met Jenny at some function or other. She was one of the promotion girls – good-looking, well-groomed, presentable, and four or five years older than me. She worked for Birmingham City Council during the day and was trying to earn a few extra quid in the evenings so she could buy a house. She was a vivacious, good-looking girl who liked a drink. I fancied her, thought she was in some way worldly, and we married soon after, in a church, with a reception at the Holiday Inn. I supposed at the time that I loved her but in reality I didn't know any better.

It's sad to report that even though we spent a long time together and had three children, I knew quite soon that our relationship wasn't right. We argued and there was often tension between us. I often wondered whether she saw me as some kind of way out, even though I was never quite sure what she was looking to escape from. Over the years, I kept hoping things would improve: I left her four times before we finally divorced.

In the meantime, I'd moved to Sheffield Wednesday and for a while I was commuting from Lichfield and occasionally staying over. By this time, I was playing for England, the England U21 team and England B, so I was a recognisable presence and for the first time became aware of women paying attention to me. Although I had the occasional dalliance I was determined to make the relationship with Jenny work, even though I was already aware of its fault lines. I was quite traditional in that sense; my mum and dad had imprinted on me a respect for marriage and I didn't want them to see my own as a failure.

Then I met a girl called Cheryl (not her real name) at a local golf range where I was drinking with David Hirst and Chris Waddle. Her dad ran a soft drinks company and we saw each other whenever things got bad between Jenny and me, which was quite often. We hit it off straightaway and even though we spent three or four years together, I don't think there was ever a sense that it would become a permanent arrangement. We had good fun, we liked each other, and I suppose we understood each other. All the same, I had a lot of respect for Cheryl. When the press got wind of our relationship they offered her good money for a lurid story, which she refused. She also had a boyfriend but that didn't work for me, and so she jettisoned him.

I know this sounds very hypocritical on my part, even selfish, but it is what it is.

At heart, I am an old-fashioned romantic and despite my situation with Jenny, I was, and am, a backward looking, conservative man. Despite what was happening in my life, my dad's principles – be immaculate, be tidy, be respectful, always be on time, always want to be in work, always be well-mannered – were buried deep inside me. I was misbehaving but misbehaving in a disciplined, high-minded sort of way, one girl at a time.

The situation with Jenny became even more complicated when I moved from Leeds to Southampton in 1997. By this time I was seeing Simone and about to call Jenny and tell her that it really was the end of the road when she phoned and told me that she was pregnant. Subsequently, she had our third child, a son, and we limped on, eventually divorcing a few years later. However, the break was not a clean one. Even though I was technically a single man, and was with Simone (and only Simone) during the two or three years following the dissolution of my marriage, I was also sleeping with my ex-wife. We continued to go on holidays together. In many ways, not much seemed to have changed, apart from the small matter of actually being married and the relative honesty of the situation.

One friend observed that I was having my cake and eating it whereas, in fact, it often felt to me that I had no cake at all and that what my life actually lacked was a fucking cake. Inside, I was yearning for a fulfilling, monogamous relationship though what I actually had was a mess of partnerships, affiliations and romances.

I continued trying to make the marriage to Jenny work. At one point, I even went to see a marriage guidance counsellor, though rather than saving or redeeming our relationship it only confirmed what I already knew: that Jenny and I must separate.

The counsellor made me write down all the reasons I still wanted to be with Jenny or, more precisely, the reasons why I wanted to go back to her. Ever diligent, always keen to please, and determined not to simply dump my marriage,

I thought hard about the answers and wrote as much as I could, covering several sheets of paper. The counsellor looked at the paper when I'd finished, taking her time, and eventually saying, 'This is very interesting'.

'In what way?'

'You've written a great deal here. It's clear that you've thought long and hard about your responses.'

'Yes,' I said, glad to have made an impression. 'I wanted to get it right.'

'There's no right and wrong in this sort of thing.'

'I was just trying to be thorough and honest.'

'And I think you have been.'

'What does that mean?'

'Well, do you know what you *haven't* said?'

'No. What?'

'There's nothing here about love. And nothing at all about your feelings. It's all about houses and children and guilt and not wanting to cause hurt.'

I couldn't argue. It was all there in black and white. It had come to the point where I felt nothing for Jenny. She had become, in the words of the counsellor, a 'habit'.

I've thought about this quite a lot over the years. Perhaps all relationships are or become in some ways mere habit? I even wondered if this tendency was more pronounced in professional sportsmen and women whose lives are necessarily framed by routine, practice and, to a certain extent, addiction. In order to be the best you can you have to lock yourself down, remain focused, and be disciplined – in your shagging and personal life, too. Even the serial shaggers in the clubs I played at had got the shagging down pat, more or less to a business-like, mechanical procedure where the room was booked, the girls arranged, and secretiveness assured. Wham, bang, thank you ma'am.

Although I was no angel, neither was I a multiple offender. All the same, I had to face the fact that in twelve or thirteen years I had gone from being a shy boy with strong feelings about marriage and leading an upright life, a boy who hid at the back of a bus, to being a married man who was messing around. Neither did I think any of my behaviour was particularly immoral. Everyone involved was a grown-up, a consenting adult. Nevertheless, my life had no centre. I never talked about it with my parents and they never gave me a lecture about it but I'm sure they disliked the situation, not least because they knew I wasn't happy.

It was getting to the point with Jenny where I felt she resented me getting any kind of attention. Every Man of the Match award or good notice was met with tight-lipped indignation from her. Did she really want me to fail? The thought crossed my mind on more than one occasion. To an extent, I was playing to prove her wrong.

In 1991 I missed the League Cup Final against Manchester United at Wembley. I'd been sent off in the previous match against Portsmouth and was automatically suspended for Wembley. I picked up a straight red card at the end of a game that was already gone. Afterwards, Ron Atkinson was furious with me.

'What did you do that for, Carlton?'

'Do what?'

'Make that fucking challenge. There was no need.'

'Yeah, well, maybe it was a bit rash.'

'You know you'll miss the cup final?'

'Fucking hell. Really?'

'Automatic suspension.'

'Fuck.'

'Twat.'

The previous year, the same thing had happened to Gary Neville but he had asked the F.A. to show leniency and they had postponed his suspension. Ron and I went down to London to see if we could cut the same deal. No dice, which pissed me off no end.

Jenny never said anything to me about it when I phoned. She hadn't bothered to find out what had happened and I didn't tell her. I'd like to say my voice was quivering with anger and self-loathing but in fact I was controlled and very cold.

'What time will you be home?'

'Soon as I can.'

'Oh. Does that mean you'll be late?'

'Not really.'

'I went shopping.'

'Really?'

'Yes. Shall I tell you what I bought?'

'If you want.'

And she did. At great length.

I was immediately angry with her. You'd have thought she might have followed the match on radio or Teletext or something, shown some interest in her husband's job. A job, incidentally, that allowed her to go to the fucking shops and buy whatever she wanted.

By the time I got home and had had a couple of drinks, I was ready to unload on her and went ballistic. Everything negative I felt about her just gushed out of me in a torrent of abuse. Perhaps I behaved unreasonably but I felt I had good cause. Perhaps I was ready to pick a fight because I would miss the cup final but that didn't matter. The rotten state of our relationship became suddenly clear to me and after I'd finished bellowing at her I went out on the piss.

Afterwards, I never forgot her indifference and lack of sympathy. The detachment. I wasn't the easiest to live with but I'd always been a good provider. Maybe too good? I had started to feel that Jenny had changed because of the money I was making and for her, it was now all about things like the cars and the holidays. Surely we owed something to each other and had an attachment that required a basic curiosity about each other's lives. But even then there was a sense of disconnection that occasionally boiled over into hostility and indifference. It wasn't that we disliked each other – that came later – more that we weren't right for one another.

Mum and dad never said anything about Jenny though I often felt they were mildly disapproving. In fact, the only comments I received about my personal life came from Harry Maney who was the coach of the Newton Albion Sunday team I played for as a kid. Harry was also a scout for QPR and took me for trials there and to Chelsea before I settled at Albion. As one of my 'second fathers', I always listened to him. For a while after I broke my leg, aged fifteen, I stopped tackling. Harry took me to one side and said I was turning into a 'fanny merchant'. He said I'd never be a footballer if I carried on like that and he set about making me aggressive and determined, effectively turning me into the awkward sod of a player I later became. Other than that, he rarely judged me, simply asking me after a game, 'How do you think you played?' He did the same when I was a professional, turning up unannounced at games (he never asked for free tickets), appearing like a ghost and asking me to rate my performance. His wife May, who eventually went blind, used to wash our kit for us. They became a little like a second family to me and I tried to look after them when I'd made a bit of money, sending them away on holiday and so on. But years later, when I was working in Dubai, recently divorced, and re-married to Lucy, I heard that Harry was ill in hospital. I went back to see him and he wasn't good. It was clear that he didn't have long to live but he asked if he could meet Lucy. They chatted for a few minutes and then he called me over and said, 'I know you're going to be all right now'. He died later that night but it's important to me that Harry met Lucy and approved of her. Recently, my mum told Lucy that she loved her 'for what you've done for Carlton'.

Mum and dad are too decent and respectful to ever say anything malicious about Jenny or interfere in my private life, but they obviously understood that I was unhappy and that something needed fixing.

I'd be interested to know if anyone has ever done a study of football marriages. It wouldn't surprise me if many ended in divorce at the fag end of a professional career. No doubt other footballers, like me, believe that if both histories had ended at the same time, it would be purely coincidental. But professional sport is a black and white business and professional sportsmen are conditioned to focus on one thing at a time. You'd have thought the end of my career and the end of my marriage might have meant a clean break and the beginning of a new life. But you'd have been wrong.

13

Not Getting It

'Nothing except a battle lost can be half so melancholy as a battle won.' Arthur Wellesley, 1ˢᵗ Duke of Wellington

Sometime towards the end of 1998, Big Ron called me.

'It's a shit line,' I said. 'Where are you?'

'Barbados.'

'No. Really where are you?'

'Barbados.'

'Don't believe you. But, ok, Barbados it is.'

'Listen, Carlton. I need your help.'

'What kind of help?'

'I want you to come and play for me again.'

'I'm all right at Southampton. I like it here.'

'Just hear me out.'

'I thought you'd retired.'

'So did I. But I've been asked to do another job.'

'Where?'

'Forest.'

'Fucking hell, Ron.'

'Yes. I know.'

At the time, Forest were having a terrible season. The glory days of Brian Clough's reign were long gone and, that season, they had just been promoted after one of their regular relegations. Now they were in danger of going straight back down again. Although they'd won two of their opening three games – one of them against Southampton – they had not won another game since and Dave Bassett had been sacked. They were nailed to the foot of the division. Even when they beat us at the Dell, it was obvious things were not right. They won more because we were crap than because they were any good. In addition, their one class player, the Dutchman Pierre van Hooijdonk, had gone on strike in order to force a move away from the club. He'd returned in October but the word was that his presence in the dressing room was corrosive. I asked Ron about him.

'It's not ideal, Carlton.'

'Is that code for it's *fucking crap*?'

'It's not code. And it is fucking crap. But it's a challenge.'

'You're telling me.'

'So will you join me?'

'I'll need to think about this. I like Southampton.'

So I thought about it and even though I was happy on the south coast, a move to Forest would, I reasoned, take me north again so I could be around my kids who were my priority. In addition, I convinced myself that a challenge like the one at Forest would be good for me and galvanise my game. And, of course, I liked working for Ron, somehow believing we could turn things round and emerge from the season as folk heroes in the East Midlands.

A week or so later, in January, I signed, more or less at the same time as Ron.

It was probably the worst professional decision I ever made. Although we had a good win at Everton, it was something of a false dawn and pretty soon a run of bad results meant we went into a catastrophic nosedive. In the first home game, Ron sat in the wrong dug-out, unable to recognise the Arsenal players who were already there as members of the opposing team. We lost 1-8 at home to Manchester United, which Ron described as a 'nine-goal thriller'. Van Hooijdonk told the press he thought Forest were being managed by Rowan Atkinson, a deliberately mischievous comment to make his position at the club even more untenable than it already was. The fans hated him and he hated them and, indeed, everything about Forest. At a time when the dressing room needed to be very together, he caused even more problems than a misfiring team has to deal with as a matter of course. There was an atmosphere of doom-laden inertia, tinged with resentment, and garnished with absurdist comedy. Winning the last three games of the season and still finishing last and five points behind the next club above us (Blackburn) was characteristically ludicrous. We were stuck in last place as early as December and never budged.

My own form was erratic. Sometimes I was good; often I was ok; occasionally I was terrible. One of those times was in the home thrashing by United, in which I played at centre back in a defence that was constantly being caught out of position. It was a humiliating experience for everyone, especially Ron, who had to endure taunts of 'Big Ron for England' from the same United fans who had been his supporters ten years earlier.

Ron's contract wasn't renewed and David Platt replaced him as manager, someone with whom, only a few years previously, I had been playing for England. Although we were fancied to come straight back up, the results were never good enough and at one point we even flirted with relegation. More to the point, Platt took a similar line with me as George Graham had at Leeds (Graham was his manager at Arsenal ... perhaps he had spoken to his protégé?), and I found myself not being selected to play, eventually being sold to Coventry soon after the new season started, where I was reunited with two of my Leeds teammates, Gary McAllister and Gordon Strachan, who was the manager. A little over a year later, I was playing for and managing Stockport County, though only after I'd squeezed in two loan spells (at Sheffield Wednesday and Watford). And less than two years after that, after a poor start to the season, I was sacked.

So, in four years I'd played for six clubs and managed one, realised (with Coventry, after the ordeal by Thierry Henry) that I was no longer able to compete at the highest level, gone into and been pushed out of management, and experienced some humbling professional reversals.

I dare say my predicament was not dissimilar to many professionals – that is, the gradual and then whirlwind unravelling of a career in which I'd been used to things more or less going my way. Suddenly, if you can call four years 'suddenly', the hard work I did and had always done, wasn't being rewarded either by appreciation or performance. It's difficult to describe what goes on inside a sportsman's head during these moments. Denial – certainly. Hope – now and then. Awareness – rarely, then often, and then eventually, constantly. Although life abruptly speeds up – Southampton to Nottingham to Coventry to Watford to Sheffield to Stockport, like an itinerary for a Ken Dodd tour – the speed is illusory and in slow motion. It's like that shot in cinema, the dolly zoom, where the camera moves in and out at the same time, creating a sense of discomfited alarm.

Somewhere inside the bursting bubble of my professional life was the bursting bubble of my marriage to Jenny. This had been shored up by money, inertia, laziness, fear, social propriety, habit, routine, the delight of having children (the latest of whom was my son, Jordan), familiarity, and not knowing what was meant to happen next. Shored up by many things, in fact, though not love. Certainly not love.

Jenny knew this, too. And then, finally, the pretence – good-natured and functional as it was for much of the time, and as it probably is for many marriages – became too much to bear. She called me into the conservatory and said she wanted to go back to Birmingham, to be near her family and her friends, though what she also meant, of course, was to be further away from me. She said something like, 'Our time's up' and I couldn't not agree with her. So we opened a bottle of champagne and talked about it.

At this point, the only thing we disagreed about was her moving back to Birmingham. I argued that that the children were born in Sheffield and felt at home there. Jenny agreed and we laid down some ground rules about the future, in particular about the possibility of meeting someone else. If that happened, we would withhold the information from the kids until we both agreed the time was right.

Neither of us wanted the house in which we were living and on which we had spent so much time and money trying to create a family home. It was put on the market and I gave her the deposit for a house in Sheffield. In addition, our assets were equally split between us and I paid her maintenance. I was aware at the time that as my playing career was coming to an end it was unlikely I would be earning the same kind of money for much longer. Better to take stock now and pay her what I was worth rather than risk a settlement that might not be feasible or possible in the future. I certainly didn't want to be tied to the sort of maintenance payments that were calculated on my earnings as a Premier League footballer when I would not be a Premier League footballer for much longer. And fuck knows what was round the corner. Football was all I'd known. Getting more or less what I'd wanted was all I'd known. So in addition to paying maintenance to her and the children (for things like school fees), plus a lump sum for the children, which was part of a 'clean break settlement' protecting me from any future court actions, I also gave her a lump sum from my pension.

At first, it all seemed amicable. Jenny found a house in Sheffield she wanted. We went on holiday together, as a family. She and I slept in the same bed and even fucked in the same bed. The kids seemed happy enough. The atmosphere was friendly. At one point, she asked if I thought there was any possibility of us getting back together again. Despite enjoying time with her and being tempted by the sense of us being a family, I'd made up my mind and didn't want to go back to the hollow convenience of our marriage. As far as I was concerned, the reason why relations were so good-natured was precisely because we were *not* married.

And so we shuffled along like this for a couple of years, not quite a family though sometimes giving a passable impression of being one. Jenny seemed content with her lump sum plus maintenance, plus the promise of another payment when she hit fifty-five.

Then the house she had wanted – or said she'd wanted – fell through. Her solicitors dragged their heels and the property was lost. Jenny ended up going back to Birmingham, which I now suspect was what she wanted all along, and taking the children with her. I didn't see them as much as I wanted. It was bad enough not seeing the girls but especially difficult not being able to watch Jordan growing from a baby into a small boy.

Around this time, I met Lucy. I sort of knew her from the school run where we'd chatted and eyed each other up while waiting for our kids outside the school gates. I liked her and I fancied her. Subsequently, we met each other by accident in a pub. Both of us had just come out of a long-term relationship so I asked her out. I was drunk but I knew that I liked her. A lot. She said no, another liaison was the last thing she needed at that time, but I gave her my number anyway.

Time passed.

Three months later she called.

I can still remember what she said. 'Against my better judgement, I have decided to call you. Do you still want to go out for a drink?'

I did – and almost immediately I knew that I wanted Lucy. She was smart (a teacher with a degree in psychology) and pretty and sensible. But I was still clinging to the strange set-up with Jenny, still imagining myself as a family man, even though it was a deluded and convenient fantasy. Lucy and I fell in love and yet I couldn't break free from the temptations of kith and kin, nearest and dearest, and all the rest of it. Then I pissed her off by further indulging my persistent dreams of domestic attachment by going on holiday with Jenny to Portugal.

This lasted all of two days before I realised what a tit I was making of myself.

I said to Jenny that I couldn't stay with her in Portugal.

'Why not?'

'I just can't.'

'Where will you go?'

'Back to England.'

I can't remember whether I told her I would be going back to Lucy or whether I just buggered off and let her work it out for herself. But whatever was said, Jenny worked out the reasons pretty quickly and her attitude to me changed.

Early evidence of a shift in her demeanour towards me emerged over a property I was buying in Spain. I was £110,000 short of the asking price and Jenny, flush from the divorce settlement and, at that time, still friendly, offered to lend me the money. Initially, I declined, though after considering the matter I went back and gratefully accepted.

Then, I presume when she worked out the degree of commitment that had developed between Lucy and I, Jenny abruptly asked for the money back. She took it to court and I was given ten days to find the money plus, for good measure, several thousands of pounds interest. I couldn't find the money in time and the bailiffs arrived at the house where Lucy and I were living.

In the end, though only after Lucy came to court with me so the judge could see for himself that I was living respectably, I was given another thirty days to find the cash.

Newspapers carried the story and, of course, made me out to be a tight-fisted and duplicitous arsehole, while Jenny was portrayed as the wronged mother just trying to move on with her life. 'He has treated me very badly,' she told one newspaper, 'and has taken advantage of my goodwill. All I want is my money back so I can get on with things.' A photo of her holding a child and looking forlorn accompanied the article. The assumption was that the child was ours. In point of fact, it was her brother's daughter. In addition, there was a provocative line in the piece saying that the money was 'for our children's future'. The implication was obvious: Carlton Palmer is a shit and is trying to cheat his family out of their money; Carlton Palmer has stolen money from his family; Carlton Palmer doesn't care about his family; Carlton Palmer is a *bad man*.

More court cases arrived. At first, it was mostly about money. 'I'll see you in the gutter,' was one of the things Jenny said to me around this time. And then things became acrimonious. I may have cheated on my wife and I may have sometimes drunk too much, but I'd always been a good provider. This wasn't about money. This just seemed like an attempt to humiliate and hurt me.

***

I walked into the room and sat down. It was quiet in there and there was a hollow, institutional echo to my footsteps as I tried to make myself comfortable. A nondescript table and a nondescript chair. I sat down. Opposite, three more identical nondescript chairs of the kind you'd find in an office. No colour in the room. Everything a kind of beige. No windows, either. The only decoration, if you could call it that, was a camera high up in the corner. I looked up at it and stared at the lens, knowing I was being watched, I was tempted to smile.

Though, of course, that was out of the question.

A few minutes passed. Knowing you are being watched though not knowing by whom … it causes a kind of self-conscious paralysis, a shutting down, a turning inwards. I continued to sit, feeling awkward, wondering what to do with my hands, my feet, every movement I made somehow magnified in my mind, as if I was imagining seeing myself as I knew others must be seeing me.

In moments like this, there is also a kind of stillness where the topsy-turvy nature of life suddenly coalesces and seems momentarily uncomplicated and lucid. I had always been used to getting what I wanted, or rather having an aim and then, mostly through hard work, achieving it. I thought I knew myself and what I wanted. I wanted to play football and make money for my family. So how had it come to this? I was about to no longer play football, I was in the middle of not having a family, and the relationship between money and family, which used to be so straightforward, was now in disarray. And now, knowing what I thought I wanted, possessing that degree of self-knowledge, was suddenly loathsome. All of a sudden, I knew myself too well. And I couldn't stand knowing about myself; it made me unhappy. Knowing the person who desired the things he wanted disturbed me. But so did not getting the things I wanted. I was fucked both ways.

Then the door opened and my kids came in. There was a moment of embarrassed inertia while we looked at one another – how could we behave normally in this environment? – and then, almost in unison, we thought, 'Fuck it', and just got on with it. We moved towards each other, hugged and chatted, and tried to enjoy the short time we had. All the same, it was like a fucking prison visit.

Afterwards, one of the social workers from Birmingham Social Services, whose building we were in, and under whose jurisdiction a court had ruled was the only place I could see my children, said it was clear I had a loving relationship with them. And after another trip to the courts, a different ruling was made, which allowed them to travel every other weekend to see me in Sheffield.

Jenny took me to court in order to stop me seeing the kids citing my drinking. Jenny took me to court to forbid me from having joint custody of the kids. Jenny took me to court for not repaying a sum of money I admitted owing to her. Jenny seized every opportunity she could to take me to court. I got used to going to court. I learnt what to wear, what to say, and when to say it. I was awarded joint custody.

And all the while, through all the court cases, I was footing the bill. My capital – what was left of it after the 50-50 split with Jenny – was being slowly wiped out. And somewhere along the way I stopped playing football and went into management, bringing in significantly less money.

And the kids were suffering. They didn't know what was happening or who to believe. Slowly, gradually, bit by bit, the life I had built for myself was disintegrating. And my usual solution to adversity – hard work plus persistence – was no longer effective.

I fell into a depression and contemplated suicide. Not seriously (I don't think) but still solemnly enough to think about the various methods available to me. I became lethargic and would sit for hours on end not doing very much but thinking about what it would be like to not exist.

I had always thought I was invincible, bulletproof.

That changed.

And how.

14

What Could Go Wrong?

'I wouldn't say I was the best manager in the business. But I was in the top one.' Brian Clough

You've worked for a number of managers. How many is it? Ten? More? Less? Some of them were good and some of them were shite. You think you've been gathering knowledge and experience. That you know what it takes to be a good manager. That in a sense your entire career has been aimed towards the moment when you hang up your boots and become the man in charge. The Boss. The Gaffer. Furtively, and perhaps without even knowing it, you've been squirreling away expertise and worldliness about the job. Instinctively, you know what to do. You've been a player, you've been managed – ergo, you know how to manage. You've heard how Brian Clough used to keep it simple. You've heard Des Walker talk about how Clough would unlace his boots and tenderly prise them off his feet after playing well for Forest. You've heard how Arsene Wenger manages to be both close to and yet remote from his players. You like the way Harry Redknapp's teams played. You admire Joe Royle's toughness. You know all the tricks – about bollocking someone when they're least expecting it, about putting an arm round someone when they've made a mistake, about sometimes saying nothing at all. You start off wanting to be Alex Ferguson. In your head you'd settle for being Sam Allardyce. And you're afraid of being Carlton Palmer. At least until 'Carlton Palmer' has been successful. Whatever that means. But most all you know that you need respect. Being liked isn't important. Being held in some kind of regard is. That's what everyone says. That's what you've seen. That's what you've learnt. If the players don't respect you they won't do what you tell them. They won't play for you. And if they won't play for you, you haven't got a team. So you think you've got half a chance at Stockport. You join them as player-manager. You've played to a level that the current players have never achieved, so you feel straightaway that they must respect the England caps, the long career at the highest level, and the cups. The track record. They might hate Carlton Palmer the man with his opinions and his mouth and his attitude but who gives a monkey's arse about that when you've got their respect? And the chairman? Brendan. Brendan Elwood. You like him. You get on well with him and he seems to have the good of the club at heart. He is putting £750,000 of his own money into Stockport every six months. He loves the place. It's his club. He owns everything, even the training ground. Trouble is, the team are in the shit. Look like they're going to be relegated. You join in November. The previous manager has been let go. Stockport are eight points adrift. You look at the players. You look at the club. You look at Brendan Elwood. You look at yourself. Yeah, you think. We can get out of this. Already Stockport is 'we'. Before I'd even signed a fucking contract. We can get out of this. I can get them out of this. I can get us out of this. You genuinely believe it, too. The chairman isn't even putting pressure on you. We talk about what might happen if we go down. I don't think we will go down but, you know, there's a chance. We ought to talk about it. Just in case. He says, 'Well, yes. If we go down, we go down. What then?' And you say pay off the big players who are on unrealistic contracts. Develop the young players. Put your faith in youth. We'll become a lean, hungry young side. Carlton Palmer will lead from the front. He will lead these youngsters from the front. He will use his experience and his nous and his belief in hard work to drive the team forwards. You believe that, too. In your mind's eye, you see a well-drilled, respectful, hard-working team of young men. They are obedient but have a swagger. They are embellished with a bit of quality. You will find that quality. You will be responsible for finding, nurturing and embellishing it. You might have to pay for it but all being well Brendan will put his hand in his pocket. He understands. They, these players, will do anything for you. Promotion? Yes. Cup run? Probably. Success (whatever that means)? Undoubtedly. You will be clear, concise and coherent in all that you do. The chairman will buy into that. The players will buy into what you want to do. The players will back you up. Nobody can challenge you. That is important. People can ask questions but only in the right way. They will understand this. It's part of the culture you will instil. Nothing can stand in the way of the team. You remember something at Leeds. Thursdays. Thursday was always working on set-pieces. The manager wanted zonal marking. You questioned the manager. You asked him how the fuck zonal marking was going to stop someone big, like, say, Tony Adams? But you ask respectfully. And the manager replies respectfully. He explains. And he's right. You challenged him in a respectful way. The whole thing is an example of mutual respect. You will introduce zonal marking at Stockport. No doubt someone will challenge you and you will explain, just as the manager at Leeds had explained to you. No one can take the piss. If the manager allows someone to take the piss, then everything turns to piss. Ferguson knew that. He got rid of the piss-takers. And when Cantona took the piss at Leeds, the manager moved him on. Cantona needed to be at a club the size of Manchester United. He needed to feel a bit intimidated in order to not take the piss. Valuable lessons, these. Tucked away. Stored. Soon they would be passed on. Stockport would benefit from all this experience. You would get changed in your office. Not with the other players. Keep a bit of distance. You would be playing as well as managing. So important to retain a little detachment. You discuss all this with Brendan Elwood, who seems like a good man. You get on with him. He asks you if you're up to the challenge. You have no doubts. You even bring in your friend, Kevin Richardson – *Rico* – with whom you played at Southampton. You know he's a good coach. He also balances you off. More measured, more political. He doesn't want you to lose the young players. He will coach the team during the week and you will do tactics on Thursday or Friday. What could go wrong? A young player-manager with a clear plan and a point to prove. What could go wrong? A supportive and understanding owner. Some decent young players. What could go wrong? On the first day – *the very fucking first day* – your star player tells you he wants to leave. He says he wants to leave to play in the Premier League. You tell him you want him to stay. We have a heated argument. The star player downs tools and won't train. You tell him he's still under contract and you want him to play, he will fucking play. What could go wrong? The manager at Blackburn Rovers calls you about your star player. He says a deal has already been done. It's not enough money for the star player but the manager at Blackburn says it doesn't matter. The deal has been done. He's worth a million quid but Blackburn are only offering £500,000. Almost immediately, the manager at Blackburn tells me he will sell him on. Yet another deal has been agreed. You tell the manager at Blackburn to fuck off and put down the phone. In the end, the star player goes to Sheffield Wednesday. Sheffield Wednesday are not in Premier League. They are in the First Division with us. And not too far above us, either. But the star player is content to go there because they offer him the most money. What could go wrong? You're eight points adrift. You draw your first game against Watford. Then, in the next game, you score the winner against Norwich. The start of something new. Something big. Then reality kicks in. Alex Ferguson told me that unless you become a manager you don't know what it takes. And you can't always be honest with the public. You can't tell them about reality. They don't want to know about reality. But what was reality? What could go wrong? So we lost the next game 0-5 at Sheffield Wednesday. What could go wrong? And then we started to lose games. We couldn't stop losing games. Eleven in a row. A club record. What could go wrong? You try everything. You shout. You encourage. You change the team. You try different tactics. You train harder. You tell the players to relax. You tell them to play with more intensity. You tell them to keep it simple. You tell them to keep possession. You tell them to press high up the field. You tell them to drop deeper. What could go wrong? We keep losing. We don't win again until March 5th. 1-0 at home to Bradford. What could go wrong? We get relegated. Even so, we beat Sheffield Wednesday in the penultimate game of the season. Too late to do any good but the ex-star player doesn't get a kick. You tell him that he isn't good enough for the Premier League and never will be. He tries to get physical with you but it doesn't work. You bully him out of the game. 'I'm 37 years old,' you tell him, 'and you're letting me walk all over you. Cunt.' What could go wrong? The phone in the office doesn't work. The local press are starting to get at you. What could go wrong? One of the players is having marriage problems. Another one thinks he's playing out of position. Two just aren't up to it but you're stuck with them. What could go wrong? You find the only enjoyment in the job is the training. Gradually you come to realise that you hate match days. Slowly you understand that you can't contribute as much as you thought, either as a player or the manager. What could go wrong? The time between games passes too quickly. It seems like nothing more than a brief pause before the next defeat. Defeat after defeat after fucking defeat. What could go wrong? You try to remain positive but people aren't looking you in the eye any more. You start to wonder whether you can manage. You start to wonder whether you can manage anything ever again. You start to wonder whether you can manage not being able to manage. You start to wonder whether you should even be playing. You start to wonder if you've shot your bolt as a player. What else could go wrong? Your marriage has fallen apart and you are having financial problems and yet somehow you've got to set the right tone. Somehow you've got to get the players on your side.

Somehow you've got to be strong with them. Somehow you've got to earn their respect. What could go wrong? So you're relegated and Brendan sticks by you and you make plans for next season. You convince yourself that the plan was always to be relegated, to offload the big players and their expensive contracts, and to put your faith in youth. So that's what happens. Plus, you buy some good players, including Luke Beckett and Rickie Lambert. You finish the season in eighth place. Promising signs. The young players are beginning to show promise. There are rumours that your job is under threat. You tell the players before the game at Northampton that if we lose the game it could be the end of the road for you. You are then sent off in the first half. Rico can barely look at you as you lope past the dugout, angry and dejected. Rico tells you to 'fuck off' when you try to give a talk at half-time. Then the fuckers, the ten-man team fuckers, come out and play as if their fucking lives depended on it. Rico tells you that all he did was remind them that they owed everything to you. You're so pumped up you could kiss each one of them. What could go wrong? The next season starts badly. The chairman sells the club to a man called Brian Kennedy who has made his money in home improvement and double-glazing. You know there's going to be trouble when all he can talk about during your first meeting is the cut glass on his fucking boat in fucking Marbella. Over the next few years under Kennedy's ownership the football club plummets towards oblivion. What could go wrong? The next season – your third – starts badly. Even so, in the last five matches you only lose one, drawing three and winning the other one. And the team is young but developing. You are sacked and a new manager is appointed. He costs £75,000 per year and will be cheaper than you. The club issues a statement saying that you have taken the club as far as you could and that you can be proud of what you have achieved in a difficult period. In other words, fuck off. What could go wrong? Your time at Stockport has flashed past. So frenetic has it been that you have come to see yourself as powerless and disembodied, almost as another person. A 'you' rather than an 'I'. Despite being caught up in the club, you have at the same time been remotely observing your vulnerability to circumstances, events and happenings. You wonder if all managers feel the same. Whether any of them feel as if they're settled and at the centre of their worlds. What else could go wrong? There's a problem with the pay-off as Kennedy tries to shear you from the club on the cheap. You don't accept his terms and the settlement goes to court. The new chairman tried to prove mismanagement of funds and the club. The judge throws it out before lunch on the first day. The new chairman has to pay full compensation to all the staff. What else could go wrong? You haven't worked for ten months while the mess is sorted out. When it's sorted, you do some work for the BBC. Then Keith Haslam, the chairman at Mansfield Town, contacts you. He has had a problem with his manager, Keith Curle, who was – wrongly, it turned out – accused of bullying a youth-team player. In the meantime, Curle has been suspended. The chairman asks if you'll take over. You think about it. You think about it very hard. And then you take the job, initially for one game (a cup tie), and then on a more permanent basis. What could go wrong? The previous season, the team had reached the play-offs. The players and the supporters have unrealistic expectations. It was a purple patch. A time when everything clicked for a bunch of players who had been together for a while. Not a fluke but an anomaly. You understand that there's luck in being a manger. Timing is important. Being in the right place at the right time. Already you suspect this could be the wrong place at the wrong time. What could go wrong? Rico can't join you. His wife was ill so you advertised for a coach and appointed Peter Shirtliff, with whom you'd played at Sheffield Wednesday. A good enough coach but, as it turned out, a disastrous appointment. What could go wrong? To prove a point, you take the players out boozing and tell them that if they can drink as much as you and keep up with you in training the next day, then they have your permission to have a drink whenever they feel like it. They fail on both counts. Point proven. Even so, you're not sure whether this has brought them closer to you or driven them away. What could go wrong? As you do every week, you organise your team for a game based on what you know about the opposition. On one occasion, when the teams are announced, they have set up their team in a completely different way. You are convinced someone has leaked information. You are enraged and shout at the players. You lose some of them but are nevertheless convinced that one of them has betrayed you. The game is lost and there is now wariness between you and the players. (Later, it turns out the leak had come from a journalist.) What could go wrong? You sign a player who can score goals but he can't settle and after three or four days he wants to leave. What could go wrong? The team starts the new season badly. Soon you are bottom of the league. The whole fucking league. The supporters, who never liked you, now turn against you. You're not sure about the players and you feel the coach doesn't support you and wants your job. Time moves too quickly again. A familiar feeling. You are not in control. Games and training hurtle past. If only everything would slow down, let you take stock, make a plan. But this time, you've got no fight left in you. The sense of being on the outside of things, of being peripheral, is exaggerated by your divorce. You're not seeing your kids. You believe that you should get rid of your coach and get on with the job. But you've got nothing left to give. You resign. The chairman, your friend, wants you to stay. All the same, you've had enough. You suspect everyone is relieved. You'll give them what they want. You'll go quietly. You go gently into the good night.

15

Oasis

'Get away from it all! Come to Dubai.' Online travel advertisement

During the times I was managing Stockport and Mansfield, my divorce to Jenny was finalised. But rather than drawing a line under our relationship and enabling us to be legally disentangled, the divorce only made me more miserable. The financial settlement we had agreed on, eventually, whereby I gave her a one-off payment, which was designed to ensure that unrealistic and unsustainable quantities of money were not expected after I'd stopped playing, did not have the intended effect of making relations between us businesslike. Nor was contact straightforward and amenable.

The settlement itself took a while to sort out. Jenny was convinced, for example, that I was hiding assets in offshore accounts. This took a year or so to deal with before it was accepted that I had nothing of the sort. Court cases in Birmingham were adjourned because more information was needed. Each postponement cost me thousands.

Sometimes, when we arranged for her to hand over the kids at a halfway point between Birmingham and Sheffield, usually at the services, they would be late. I made the point in court that if I didn't comply with a Court Order by, say, not making a maintenance payment, the bailiffs turned up. But if Jenny was in breach of an order by not making the kids available to me at the agreed time, then I was simply told to report it to the police.

In many respects Jenny was and is a good mother. That's not the issue as far as I'm concerned. But in my opinion, she was not allowing me to be a good father. Or to be the kind of father I wanted to be. By hurting me I felt she was also hurting them. Not only were her attempts to gain money from me bound to have an effect on my ability to provide for our kids, it was also going to deprive them of the kind of father they needed. For this behaviour, exhibited time and again in the years following our divorce, I will never be able to forgive her.

Quite recently, Kelly moved out of the family home and into a house Jenny owned (but had been bought with my money) and agreed to pay rent, which I coughed up for. In effect, I was paying money to Jenny to cover our daughter's rent in a house which I had bought. Although it was all quite legal, it was the kind of crazy situation that seems to have snowballed since our divorce

Over the few years since we divorced, the mood between us has become attritional. Now I am the first person – actually, probably not the first but certainly amongst the first wave of grumblers – to understand that I am not the easiest person to live with. I can be opinionated, truculent, and moody. I like a drink. I inhabit routine. I tend to see things in very straightforward, clear-cut ways. Yes. I know these things. But I am also pretty honest and ethical. And, most important, or at least what should be most important so far as Jenny is concerned, I have always tried to do the best for our kids. Without spoiling them, and by trying to give them a framework within which I would give them financial help, I always came through on my promises for them. I helped them with property, cars and education. I took them on holidays. Whenever they asked for it, I gave them candid and sincere advice. I don't think I ever tried to set them against Jenny, who I know they loved and in so many other ways had been an important and loving figure in their lives.

All this was going on while I was managing and pretty soon afterwards not managing Stockport and Mansfield. In-between times, I was working for the BBC, though the work there also began to stall. By 2006, I was financially stretched and then the economic turndown tied up all my money in unsellable assets. In addition, I had no guarantee of work. Plus I was knackered and worn to a frazzle by the strains of management and the grinding erosion of Jenny's behaviour.

In short, I'd had enough.

It was also around this time that I started travelling to Dubai. My sister Sharon lived in the Emirates so I knew the city a bit from visiting her. Lucy and I also went on honeymoon there. It was during one of these trips that we spoke about the future.

'What do you *want* to do?' she asked.

A simple question though actually a very difficult one to answer.

'I don't know,' I replied.

'Well, think about it.'

I thought about it. All I'd ever known was football. All I'd ever wanted to be was a footballer. I liked football. Sometimes it seemed like football was the only thing I did like. Lucy could sense what I was thinking. 'Maybe you should carry on playing,' she said. 'You gave up too early.'

'For fuck's sake, Lucy,' I said, 'I'm forty-fucking-two years old.'

'You can still play. You know you can. You're fitter than men half your age.'

She had a point. Well, half a point. And in fact I was still receiving offers from clubs in the Championship. If I really wanted to, I could pull on my boots again and play at a reasonably high level. I'd probably enjoy it. But, somehow, it just didn't feel right. I'd made a decision. There was no going back.

'No. I'm done,' I replied.

'You'd better find something else – and quick. Otherwise you'll drive yourself and everyone else up the wall. Especially everyone else. And in particular, me.'

Part of the trouble was not only that I had never wanted to do anything else except play football but I had never known anything else *but* football. I didn't have a trade or a profession or an education that could lift me out of the game. Although I was amongst the generation of footballers that preceded the current one where kids are intensively coached from a very young age and are never allowed to lead a normal adult life, it is still fair to say that in some ways I never learned to become a man. Like so many footballers, I had acquired the trappings of a successful grown-up life without ever having properly inhabited the adult world. Not *everything* was done for me and I don't believe I ever had too much money, so I never believed I could do whatever I wanted without having to face up to it … but an air of unreality did hang over me. How would I now find a place in the world?

This, of course, is a problem that all retiring sportsmen and sportswomen have to face. I suppose it used to be easier. I mean, in the days when being a footballer was more like a normal job and the players were part of a community. They used to catch a bus to the ground with the supporters. Afterwards, they would share a drink with them. Often, a team would be composed almost entirely of men who had been locally born and bred. When these players retired from playing, they were already embedded in a community that would find a place for its retired footballers. Pub landlord, garage owner, shopkeeper, bookie – football had merely been a temporary excursion for that generation. They were not isolated or excluded from society. Today, clubs are so keen to sign young players that they do everything for them. When they finish playing they discover that they've been living in a bubble. Daily life is a tedious puzzle for them. They have no hinterland to fall back on. And how do you deal with the reality of no longer doing the only thing you've ever done or been able to do? The knack of playing football isn't often integrated into anything much resembling a personality, so players must learn to function socially and emotionally, to get their bearings in the world.

There are some high profile examples of ex-players who have come badly unstuck (Paul Gascoigne and the temporarily homeless Kenny Sansom come to mind) but whatever happens, it's a difficult void to fill. For years, you've been submerged in routine and not having to think how to lead a life other than a footballing one. Each day is mapped out for you – say, Monday and Tuesday training; Wednesday winding-down; Thursday for tactics; Friday rest and final preparations for a game; Saturday the game itself – and you're even told what to wear, what to eat, and what time to go to bed. For fuck's sake, someone even puts out your kit for you, like your mum used to when you were a little boy. You get addicted to the routine; you get addicted to the adrenalin rush; you get addicted to the money; in short, you are addicted to football. You get used to the money, often living to your means or beyond them. You never think about 'afterwards'. And when it's over, you're unprepared. Caught with your pants down. Even when – if – you get a job, whether it's driving a taxi or working in an office or starting a business or whatever, there's often an unhappiness and a sense of loss. Relationships fail. Marriages collapse. Drink gets a grip. Gambling replaces the buzz of playing.

It's not all gloom. I played with Craig Shakespeare at Sheffield Wednesday. Now, Craig is an even-headed person though even he was never going to put away enough money for 'afterwards'. So he got a job in insurance, which made him unhappy. He missed football. His wife, Karen, spotted the warning signs and persuaded him to do his coaching badges. Craig has since gone on to success, first winning the Premier League at Leicester, as assistant to Claudio Ranieri, and then being promoted to manager when Ranieri was sacked.

Craig's example is an interesting and, in the end, happy one. But it is not typical. So I knew about the dangers of packing it in and turning my back on the game. In a sense, the jobs at Stockport and Mansfield, the player-manager role, even the occasional punditry, were all substitutes for the real thing. A gradual descent. A slow parachute jump away from the game and the only way of life I knew that also gave me the sense that I was still, somehow, attached to it.

But what now? I was forty-two and still a relatively young man. Was I really even more difficult to live with than usual? Were there worrying signs of bewilderment and having lost my bearings? Fuck knows. But Lucy was right. In time, I'd drive everyone mad. Especially her.

We had this conversation while we were in Dubai on one of our occasional visits. I liked the place. The weather was hot, the hotels were very comfortable, the food was fantastic, and the beaches were a good place to unwind. Contrary to expectations and what I'd heard about Dubai, I could even drink. So long as you did your drinking in certain places – and there were quite a few 'certain places' – and did not make a public display of any drunkenness, there were no problems in that respect. In some bars, you would even find Emirati men drinking, too. At the time, it was odd seeing a group of Arab men, all wearing flowing white thawbs, holding pints of Guinness or knocking back shorts. But they did.

After years of domestic stress and the problems at Stockport and Mansfield, it was something of an oasis. I looked forward to my trips to the UAE without ever considering that I might actually live there.

Then things began to change. Ray Reid, who produced *TEN Sports*, offered me work as an analyst, commenting on Premier League and UEFA Champions League games. The pay was good and with the infrequent work I was still getting from the BBC, I was able to fly quite easily between England and Dubai, fulfilling job obligations in both countries.

And then something even stranger happened. Ray told me about David May, the ex-Manchester United defender, who had been offered a job at Repton School, but then pulled out. Repton was a new school in Dubai, a version of the famous old English public school in Derbyshire, whose alumni included Roald Dahl, Jeremy Clarkson, C.B. Fry, and Bunny Austin. He said that the Headmaster, David Cook, was interested in talking to me and before I knew it I was being interviewed.

I liked David, a rotund, affable cartoon of a man with a passion for food, drink, sport and Leicester City, not necessarily in that order. He offered me a job setting up a sports academy at the school and I was impressed by his enthusiasm and vision. He was also offering a generous salary, it must be said, which at the time was also very attractive to me.

All the same, I wasn't sure it was the right thing. Although I was keen to get out of England on a more or less permanent basis, thus bringing to an end the nagging control that Jenny exerted and the persistent unpleasantness she inflicted on my life, it would have meant leaving Lucy in England. At least for the time being and until she could sort out a job. Neither would I be able to see the kids as often as I liked.

I was undecided.

We talked.

'You should go,' Lucy said. 'It would solve so many things. And being in England just makes you unhappy.'

'I'm not unhappy.'

'Angry, then.'

'Really?'

'Yes.'

'I'm angry?'

'Borderline psychotic,' she laughed.

Lucy has a degree in psychology so she knew what she

was talking about. All the same, I wasn't having her label me as deranged, even if she did mean it as a joke.

'Bugger off.'

'Bugger off yourself.'

'What? Bugger off to Dubai?'

'Yes.'

I considered. Lucy always talked sense. Well, more sense than me.

'I'd miss you.'

'It's only six hours. Direct to Manchester. I'll get over there as often and as soon as I can.'

'I don't know, Luce. It's a school.'

'So?'

'I've never worked in a school.'

'You didn't hate school when you were *at* school.'

'That's not the point.'

'And just think what it would have meant to you as a schoolboy.'

'What do you mean?'

'Having an England football player as your football coach.'

'For fuck's sake, Lucy. You're not going to tell me I should give something back, are you?'

'Yes I fucking well am. You should give something back.'

I'm not sure that I made my decision based on any sense that I was being public-spirited, but a pleasant lifestyle plus money plus the illusion of being kind-hearted was a winning combination.

So I joined the staff at Repton, escaping from England, earning a decent wedge, and (of course) giving something back.

Almost immediately, and contrary to my expectations, I

was enjoying it. I liked being part of a team again. I liked the routine. I liked finding ways to coach kids, some of whom might have had two left feet. I liked the way of life. I liked combining work at the school with my stints on television. And when the Head of P.E., suspicious of me and obviously anxious that I wouldn't pull my weight, assuming that I was an overpaid diva, asked me to pick up the bibs at the end of a training session, I found I even liked picking up the fucking bibs. Or more likely, I liked proving him wrong. I'd always enjoyed proving people wrong. I wanted to show him that I was no prima donna and was quite prepared to roll up my sleeves and get on with things.

The drill and repetition of school life worked for me. I enjoyed having to be at a certain place at a certain time. The rhythm of the school day and its defined term-times suited me. Uniforms, codes of behaviour, discipline, designated objectives, camaraderie, banter … in some ways, it was a bit like being at a football club. Maybe footballers are really just children? They have to be controlled, reassured and given a proper framework to work within. I can't say the thought didn't cross my mind.

I stood by the door every morning and greeted pupils as they arrived at school, checking their uniforms and welcoming them. Meanwhile, the football teams were being well coached and getting a reputation in Dubai. They won tournaments and impressed people with their polished orderliness on the field. The sports academy I directed was also developing. The facilities at the school were good and we were adding to them all the time. Extra tennis courts were built. A second swimming pool was opened. Floodlights were installed on the main pitch.

Having said that, there were also moments of madness.

On the day it was due to open, the Senior School hadn't been built. Barely started, in fact. So term was postponed by three weeks and the classrooms hurriedly constructed. We all mucked in, constructing lockers, grouting bathrooms, and lugging around wheelbarrows of building materials. I remember thinking, 'Fuck me, Carlton. Eighteen England caps later and all that hard work, and you've still ended up on a building site'.

At such times, the heat was unbearable. Standing out in the sun, you could feel the skin on any unprotected part of your body or face beginning to burn, causing a puckering, shrivelling sensation. The sun was like something out of *Lawrence of Arabia* – a vast, incandescent shimmering ball that chucked out an unrelenting heat. Naturally, no sport could be played in this climate, most football matches (for example) being delayed until late afternoon at the earliest. And in the summer, not even then. Which makes the decision to host the 2022 World Cup in Qatar, frankly, ridiculous.

I was still living and working in Dubai when the bidding process was concluded. I mean, even venturing out of one air-conditioned building and walking a few yards to another one was an exhausting, debilitating experience. And even if the playing area in the stadia in Qatar were able to be successfully air-conditioned – and I've played in places in America where this has been achieved with a degree of success – there is no way that crowds could survive the heat. When the school photo was taken at Repton, an activity which entailed doing no more than standing in the heat for up to thirty minutes, kids were fainting and keeling over. The UAE is not a place to be playing football – certainly not in the summer and at other times rarely before

5 p.m. Everyone who has worked there or even visited the area and walked more than one hundred yards in the heat knows this.

I had better be careful how I put this next bit. But what I will say is that the Emiratis are football mad and regard hosting the World Cup not merely as a privilege but a sign of how far oil-money has brought them. I will also say how much importance they attach to money and the ostentatious display of wealth. And I will add that I have experienced at first hand their conviction, often relentlessly and unscrupulously enacted, that money can buy anything. Furthermore, experience has shown them that the lofty and perhaps hypocritical principles of the West are vulnerable when those standards come into contact with cash. Anyway, during my stay in Dubai I watched as a not insignificant number of renowned footballing personalities popped up in the UAE to lend their support to Qatar's bid. As each of these made his point, the perception of Qatar as an absurd destination for a football tournament began to shift. You sensed that integrity had become an adjustable commodity. So I was not surprised when Sepp Blatter opened the envelope and announced Qatar as the winner of the bidding process to host the 2022 World Cup. It had been coming. If Dubai could build a ski-slope with real-artificial snow (there were even rumours of the city hosting the Winter Olympics), then Qatar would certainly have the balls to believe it could host the World Cup.

Be that as it may, I was enjoying myself in Dubai. The kids came to visit (with Jenny, of course), Lucy got a job and joined me, and I was able to move comfortably between my responsibilities at Repton and my work as a pundit. All was good. I was, as they say, happily retired. Dubai was doing exactly what I had hoped it would, i.e. take the heat out of the situation with Jenny and allow me to stabilise my financial situation.

And the madness of the place was as entertaining and diverting as it was preposterous. An IGCSE art exhibition in the school was dismantled because one of the pupil's paintings featured something that looked like a concentration camp, and the Holocaust was deemed to be Jewish propaganda; a pick-up side consisting of my coaching staff and a few retired ex-pros beat a combined Norwich-Swansea side at a time both teams were in the Premier League – the players' only interest was in the expensive watches they had bought in a mall; at Repton's International Day, a boy from Somalia came to school dressed as a pirate; in the life-drawing class, vaginas are routinely concealed by the judicious placement of buttons; a temporary shortage of vinegar in Dubai makes the front page of a local newspaper; two men are arrested for giving women tips about make-up and acting in 'unmanly' ways; a boy and a girl are found having sex in the school's prayer room; a local survey concludes that plastic bags are responsible for fifty per cent of all camel deaths in the region; someone starts a grass-cutting business called 'Lawns of Arabia'.

I mean, what's not to like?

Harry Redknapp and his wife Janet came over for a break and I remember having a drink with them at a hotel near the Medan racecourse. At the time, he was manager of Spurs and there was talk of him being the next England manager.

'Do you miss it, CP?' he asked.

'No,' I said. 'It's fine.'

'Really?'

'Yes. Really. Not at all.'

Harry, who lives and breathes the game, couldn't understand it.

'Come on. You must miss it a bit.'

'I don't. I'm content. That's the truth.'

'Fuck me. Well ... ok.'

I don't think he believed me. I don't think he could believe anyone who said they didn't miss football. But as I said to him when I saw his already crumpled face scrunching up even more with doubt, 'It is what it is, Harry'.

16

Square Eyes

'If a man watches three football games in a row, he should be declared legally dead.' Erma Bombeck

Dion Dublin was in Dubai to do some television work, I think on a Champions League game. However, one thing led to another and Dion couldn't make the engagement so I was asked to step in even though it was my night off and I had made other arrangements. I agreed despite knowing I would be at a wedding and probably, i.e. certainly, drunk. Nevertheless, I felt I could get through the programme without too much bother so I sobered myself up, had a shower, and headed to the studio.

The programme itself was uneventful. Despite feeling under the weather, I got through it fine. No one in the studio said anything to me before, during or after the show. No complaints were received from viewers shocked at the sight of a drunken ex-footballer slurring his words and making an arse of himself. They didn't complain because it didn't happen.

Three days later, I was called in by the company and suspended for being drunk on air.

'Someone has complained,' I was told, 'and we've

looked back at the tapes of the show and there might be something in it.'

I tried to defend myself.

'Does this *someone* work for the company?'

'No.'

'And there's just a single complaint?'

'That's right.'

'Received two days after the programme had aired?'

'Correct.'

'Sounds odd to me. It just doesn't add up.'

After a bit more of this to-ing and fro-ing, and after asking around, I learned from where the complaint was most likely to have come. It seemed that an ex-footballer who was working for a rival television company was the most likely culprit. (He denies it, by the way.) The reason? To get me pushed off the programme so he could take my place – or at least to get more airtime for himself.

Eventually, my suspension was overturned but it reminded me how much football had changed. Even though I had finished playing quite recently, there was suddenly far more money in the game and people wanted to get their hands on it. Agents, players, managers, coaching staff and now, apparently, even pundits were clambering aboard the gravy train, elbowing people aside and jostling for position. Years later, I learnt that people like Robbie Savage and Joey Barton would say inflammatory things on Twitter to increase their followings, this being the way that pundits were hired. Punditry was fast-becoming a competitive sport. This I already knew from my experiences with the BBC. The inertia of my career as a pundit for the Beeb was part of the reason I went to Dubai in the first place.

I'd always assumed I was a good pundit. I rarely sat on

the fence though I always tried to be fair, doing my best not to criticise players. From my own days as a footballer, I knew how easy it was to have a bad game, and for the media to then latch onto it and build it into something more significant than it really was. I also thought I was good at dissecting games and seeing things that viewers might miss, which I assumed was the purpose of punditry – telling people something that wasn't obvious, telling them something they didn't already know.

I was sent on a training course in Nottingham before I started with the BBC. I was told to imagine that the audience doesn't understand what's going on, to talk about systems, and to explain what was happening and how teams could counter one another. Plus, there were tips about being concise, direct and explicit. Like a schoolboy swot, I used to write everything down before going on air, even some of the expressions I might use. I was also encouraged to turn statements into questions and then, quickly, supply the answer, this (apparently) being the way to connect with viewers who felt they were being directly addressed. It also maintained a sense that I knew what I was talking about. Still, I never got the hang of this or saw the point of it, but some pundits and commentators have built entire careers around it.

The BBC was a curious place to work, an odd mixture of the formal and the relaxed, the officious and the liberal. We had a dress code (smart shirts with only the top button permitted to be undone and the cuffs buttoned; smart-casual trousers; shirts tucked in) that seemed to be more relaxed than Sky (ties and jackets were worn and more often than not, suits) but was actually, in its own way, more unvarying and conservative. The Sky pundits looked like a group of blokes who were attending a mate's wedding whereas working for the BBC always made me feel as if I was stepping into the pages of a menswear catalogue.

We were never told what to say (or, just as important, what not to say), and in that respect the BBC was quite grown-up. No swearing, obviously. And occasionally we would be told to stay away from a controversial topic that might have legal implications, the bungs scandal being the one that springs most obviously to mind. A growing trend has been the reluctance to upset managers. This is a political issue – television is very concerned that the game is perceived as being one big happy family. If the managers are on board it sort of gives television commentary a degree of credibility, an easy and accepted authority within the footballing fraternity. When I was there, there was much gnashing of the teeth about Alex Ferguson's decision not to speak to the BBC. And, as a consequence, strategies to get him in front of the cameras again were often discussed.

Friday evening, the night before the coverage of most matches, the pundits were put up at the Grosvenor Hotel in London. Usually, the team consisted of Gary Lineker, Mark Lawrenson, Alan Shearer, and Alan Hansen (from *Match of the Day*), and those who were involved with *Final Score* and *Football Focus*, a group that might include people like Garth Crooks, Martin Keown and Lee Dixon.

We'd spend Friday evening catching up, talking about football in general, and discussing the forthcoming games. It was always very genial and, yes, Lineker is as nice as he seems to be. Or at least he has always been kind and decent to me. Once, I was given his changing room by accident. It's bigger and better fitted out than the others. I didn't know it was his and without thinking I made myself at home, unpacking my stuff and generally lodging myself there. Later, we were all in the studio when Lineker appeared, red in the face and clearly angry.

'Someone's taken my fucking dressing room,' he growled.

I put two and two together. Even my maths was up to it.

'Sorry, mate,' I said. 'I think that's me. It was an accident.'

'Oh,' he replied.

'No problem. I'll go up there and move my stuff.'

Gary Lineker was not Matt Le Tissier. I'd have happily moved.

'No worries, Carlton. You stay were you are.'

'It'll only take ten minutes.'

'Really. It's ok. I've put my stuff in the other *smaller* room,' he smiled. 'I'm happy there.'

It was a relatively trivial thing but I've known so-called celebrities getting very agitated about any apparent loss of status. Lineker was quite secure in his standing and didn't need to constantly reinforce it at other people's expense. His anger effortlessly became something else, something amiable and gracious.

Television captures his charm and friendliness very well. The impudent smile, the light touch, the twinkle – these things are a part of him that he is now able to communicate with a kind of unselfconscious ease. Over the years, he has learnt to project these sides of his character very effectively. He's even managed to make a few bob selling crisps, which everyone acknowledges as an unhealthy food, even whilst appearing in the adverts as a kind of pantomime villain. His reputation is so secure that he can even make a virtue out of plugging a harmful product and presenting himself as a degenerate character. Lineker has become a kind of brand. Tinkering with it, even contradicting it, now only reinforces its underlying and perceived meaning.

But that is also what he is like. He has always made time for me, asked after the kids, given Lucy a warm hug, been generous in the studio, and offered help when he is able. The real Gary Lineker and the television Gary Lineker have become more or less the same person.

Alan Hansen was able to do much the same thing, fluently conveying the sense of a man who is intelligent (he is), can accomplish most things he puts his mind to (he can), and has a hint of steel beneath the urbane disposition (he does).

Being comfortable in front of a camera is difficult. It's not acting – well, not quite – but it's not far removed. How to convey the person you want to come across as, to control or shape people's perception of you, takes practice, a certain kind of insincerity, and the good fortune of the camera actually liking you.

Hansen and Lineker both had the knack or developed it. Alan Shearer and Mark Lawrenson both took a bit longer. Shearer is actually a funny bloke and it's taken him a while to find a way to transmit this. Working out a way to feel at ease, to literally be yourself, can be perplexing. I mean, you're *yourself* all the rest of the time, but actually performing *being yourself* is weird.

I don't think I was particularly bothered by the camera. I can't recall ever feeling nervous. The only problem I had was trying to remember not to swear. And I was always quickly into the notes I'd made in my head.

On the Saturday, everyone – including the *Match of the Day* team – would be hanging around the *Final Score* studio. While people were looking at screens and reporting various matches 'live', Lineker and co. would ask questions, scribble notes, and generally prepare for their own programme later in the evening. They wanted to know if there were any incidents that required comment, determine the running order of the games, and make sure they didn't miss anything. Though relaxed and affable, Lineker himself was very much the leader of the operation. I always felt he worked best when he was surrounded by people he could trust and it's fair to say that he had a big influence on those he worked with: if you didn't get on with Gary, you didn't get on the show. I know of at least two ex-players who didn't gel with him. Neither of them lasted long.

Hansen was one of my favourite players when I was a kid. When I was an apprentice at Albion I took tea into the Liverpool dressing room and he was fast asleep on a bench, minutes before the match. Needless to say, he had a brilliant game.

All the pundits have different characters. All are aware they have something to offer but, ah, finding a way to express that on camera is the key to success. Inevitably, and despite there being a good craic and a mutual love of football, there is also an element of rivalry. Becoming a pundit is a good way to stay in touch with the only way of life that many of us have known, to maintain a relationship with the game we love, and to earn a few bob into the bargain. Trouble is, there aren't many places up for grabs. And we are all competitive sportsmen. Beneath the chummy exteriors, there is an element of dog-eat-dog combativeness.

A few of us, including Lee Dixon and Martin Keown, were amongst those hopeful of establishing some kind of foothold within the Beeb. Lee Dixon had an immediate advantage. He played golf. More than that, he played golf with Gary Lineker. Playing golf is an important part of an ex-footballer's life, and playing golf with the right people is especially important. I tried to play golf. I wanted to play golf. I even bought a house in Portugal next to a fucking golf course so I could learn to play golf. Trouble is, I looked ridiculous playing golf. For starters, there's the golfing gear, all those pastels and patterns. It felt more like going out to a tea party than participating in a sport. Plus I can't hold a golf club for toffee. When I swing the club, it just looks wrong. Golf and me are just a bad match. It's like watching a jockey playing rugby or a sumo wrestler on a bobsleigh. The nearest I ever got to completing a round of golf was one time in Jamaica with Tony Adams. We turned the match into a drinking game and both of us got so pissed that we were thrown off the course.

I never knew for sure why I didn't push on at the BBC. No one debriefed you or gave feedback. It was too polite and gentlemanly to risk anything like a run-in. You found out you weren't getting on by not being asked back. Simple as.

There was one thing that probably counted against me.

I was reporting live on Everton versus Sunderland and one player was having a poor game. I pointed this out on air using the language of the training ground.

'He's having an absolute holocaust,' I exclaimed.

There was a momentary and shocked silence in the studio although nobody actually said anything. Then the programme jerked itself back into life and carried on as usual.

However, the producer, Niall Sloane, was furious with me and demanded that I make a public apology in the newspapers, which I duly did. It was either that or the sack. I understand, of course, that it was an unwise thing to say … but were people really thinking that I was drawing comparisons between a football player having a shit time of it and the extermination of the Jews?

Niall Sloane later went to work at ITV. He took Lee Dixon with him. And Lee Dixon also played golf with Niall Sloane.

Ok, so the holocaust comment wasn't judicious, never mind that it was made in the heat of the moment and (in my opinion) too much was made of it. But other observations I made were unfairly ridiculed and taken out of context. When I said, for example, that Peter Crouch was a 'better striker' than Zlatan Ibrahimovic I didn't mean that Crouch was a better player but a better *striker*, and his goals per game record for England proves this. I was also trying to stick up for Crouch who has received a lot of stick, much of it unjust, and much of it probably because (like me) he doesn't look much like everyone's idea of a footballer. Us ungainly ones have got to stick together.

On another occasion, I suggested that Steven Gerrard wasn't a world-class player. I knew that would cause a problem for me, as everyone else in the world seemed to think Steven Gerrard was a world-class player. They'll roll their eyes in a dismissive way, go all weak at the knees, and mutter 'Istanbul' as if his heroics in that match proved their point. But, really, we're talking here about being *world class* for fuck's sake and there aren't many players who qualify. Just being a very, very good footballer doesn't count.

And when I offered the opinion that Paul Ince was as good if not a better player than Roy Keane, the reaction was hysterical, as if I'd killed Bambi. But I've played against both of them and while they're both really good players I always found Ince more difficult. For a start, and despite the common perception of him, Ince was a genuine box-to-box player. He was just more active on a football field. Keane didn't get up and down in the way that people think. They saw his determination and his drive and just assumed they equated to all-action, blade-covering performances. Well, they fucking didn't.

So why wasn't I allowed to say these things – honest opinions that were backed up either by evidence or an informed viewpoint – without being slagged off as 'inane' or 'bitter'? Why is it that Alan Hansen, for example, can say 'You can't win anything with kids' and then sit back and relax as his misreading of the skills of Scholes, Beckham, Giggs, Butt, and the Neville brothers is turned into a fondly remembered blip? And certainly not as a sign of inanity or resentment.

Hansen, of course, is white, gets on with Gary Lineker, plays golf well, talks with an authoritative Scottish accent, and has an A level in Latin. So you don't fuck with him. As opposed to Carlton Palmer, who isn't white, looks like a dick when he plays golf, talks with a comical Brummie accent, and doesn't have any A levels. So you can fuck with him.

Television is a strange and often enigmatic middleman between football and the people who watch it, the people who used to be called simply 'fans'. Now it is more complicated than this and I was finding out that maybe my face didn't fit. Some people are able to become go-betweens or are embraced more readily as intermediaries. For whatever reason, I am not one of those people.

The ex-Manchester City manager Manuel Pellegrini is a humorous, amiable and warm man, but somehow comes across on television as reticent and hangdog, almost guilty. The apparent guilt he felt at his team's inability to always play scintillating football was seen in his television appearances. People saw it almost as an admission of wrongdoing. Carlo Ancelotti's open, relaxed manner in front of the cameras is read by many as a sign that he has nothing to hide and is in total control. At Spurs, Mauricio Pochettino's early habit of not conducting television interviews in English gave him an immediate mystique and kept the media at arm's length. Until his results did their own talking, he did not want to be distracted by having to manage his on-air character.

Thinking about all this stuff can drive you mad and maybe I should have thought about it a bit more. But all I did was turn up, think about the football, make some notes, and get on with it. Perhaps I should have managed my persona more carefully, turned Carlton Palmer into *Carlton Palmer*. But I'm not like that.

With hindsight, I think I arrived on television with too much baggage. I was perceived as the bloke who was lucky to win eighteen England caps, who didn't play football in the way people wanted football to be played. People were ready to jump on any so-called mistakes and less willing to give me the benefit of the doubt, have patience, and give me time to develop a proper identity for the television. As people in television gave time, for example, to Lineker and Shearer.

You can see them now, the pundits, all delivering versions of themselves for the television, reinforcing comforting permutations of their already familiar characters. Paul Merson's goofy stooge; Jamie Carragher's chippy, independent-minded Scouser; Phil Thompson's spirited zealot; Alan Shearer's thin-lipped ruthlessness;

Michael Owen's deadpan pleasantries. Even Paul Scholes, who famously was almost silent in front of the cameras when he was playing (though he had plenty to say while he was actually on the field), now uses his tight-lipped persona to underpin his punditry. Paul Scholes who never said a word now says quite a lot, what he says being perceived as *honest* and *principled* because it comes from a deep and silent place.

So why can't Carlton Palmer – honest, straight-talking, occasionally humorous, hard-working Carlton Palmer – do the same? Difficult to say. But there's an alchemy about it that I just don't seem to possess or that other people don't want to buy into. Television seems to heighten already existing prejudices about you and you can either polish these or try to change them. Perhaps I didn't do enough of the latter. And the former came with too much adverse baggage. You've had your moment, people seemed to be thinking. Be grateful for what you've got. *Don't push it.*

17

Mellow

'China is a great country with a great culture, populated by fascinating, industrious and talented people.' Vladimir Putin

I wanted to watch the 2016 Championship play-off final at Wembley between Sheffield Wednesday and Hull City at a bar, surrounded – if that is possible in Shanghai – by other Wednesday fans. I tweeted that I would be in The Camel at around midnight, which was when the match kicked off 'China time'. It had been pissing down all day and as midnight approached it was still pissing down. In point of fact, it had been pissing down for days. It didn't matter. I was happy enough. My team had a chance of being promoted to the Premier League and I was excited at the prospect of watching the game. By the time I arrived, I was already well-oiled. There'd been an event at school during the afternoon (plenty of beer) and afterwards a group of us had gone to a friend's flat (plenty more beer). So when I pitched up at the sports bar in the French Concession area of the city, I was already flying.

A small group of Wednesday supporters was already there. I ordered a Guinness and took my place amongst them. Like all bars in China, smoking is still permitted, so the atmosphere – smoggy, hazy, smoke-filled, murky – is like a throwback to pubs in England about twenty years ago. About the time I was still playing, in fact. It took you back.

One of the French teachers at school had told me that there is a French word for a group of smokers who meet together to form a kind of smoking club. The word, *tabagie*, was about to disappear until France enforced the smoking ban. But now it's used to describe the small groups of people huddled together outside bars, restaurants and work places, united in suffering under the ban of their favourite activity. I'm not very good with languages but I do like collecting words or phrases that might prove useful or somehow strike a chord in me. In China, I'm able to say, 'Another one of the same, please' and 'Is this Happy Hour?' but not a lot more.

There was no *tabagie* huddled outside The Camel because those that smoked were all inside, clustered together and making a right racket. Although I wanted to be amongst Wednesday fans I remained at a discrete distance, not wishing to impose myself. There's nothing antisocial about this. Fans are a different breed. The fanaticism and loyalty they show towards a club requires there is a certain distance from its players. It's the interval between the two things that allows an irrational, compulsive bond to form. If they get to know too much about a club and its players, how things really work and what people are really like, then it puts the whole set-up at risk.

I am a Wednesday supporter. I had the best years of my career as a Wednesday player. I loved playing for the team and I loved the team we had and the kind of football we tried to play. I loved the supporters and I like to think we had a good relationship. Working class people, they liked players who tried, and the one thing you could guarantee from me as player was effort. Back in the day, I would often go to the pub after a game and mix with the supporters. When I walked in, they would sing, 'We've got Carlton Palmer, He smokes marijuana ...' A few in The Camel struck up the same song as I walked in, more in fond memory, I think, than with the full-throated passion of old. I liked being at Wednesday so much and grew so fond of the area that I continued living there even when I moved on from the club. It suited me very well. The proximity to the countryside, the sense of being in a manageable city that wasn't overwhelmingly big or clogged with traffic, its closeness to family roots in Birmingham. I loved the club. I loved the city. I loved the people. By degrees, I became a Wednesday supporter. If you asked me now which club I supported I would say, without hesitation, 'Sheffield Wednesday'. But being a Wednesday supporter and being one of its ex-players is different to only being a Wednesday supporter. For me, as with all ex-players, football was a job, and this invariably takes the gilt off the game. You can't quite commit in the same way. As a kid, I supported Albion and that kind of childish enthusiasm for your hometown club is still in me. I also, of course, have soft spots for all the teams I played for and managed. I keep tabs on each club's results. Nevertheless, I am a Wednesday supporter, even if the allegiance comes with strings attached.

Standing in The Camel, with but not quite *with* the thirty or so Wednesday fans who had turned up to watch the game, many in the blue-and-white striped kit, some of the shirts twenty years old, some from the current season, I saw someone trying to take a photo of me. Instinctively, I took a step backwards and moved behind a pillar. Now, whenever someone approaches me for a chat or a photo, so long as it's done in the right way – politely and with friendliness – I don't mind. Actually, it's a kind of compliment and I don't like the way that today's footballers are cordoned off from the public, the way that they are managed and isolated, living in a strange fantasy world of their own devising – or rather, one that has been devised for them by their agents. But neither do I like sneakiness. If someone wants to take a photo then they can front up and fucking well ask.

Which is then precisely what happened. Two women found me behind the pillar, one of them holding the camera-phone, and asked if they could have a photo with me. One of them explained that her brother had seen my tweet about being in The Camel. He was also a Wednesday supporter but lived in another Chinese city and had asked his sister to come along and get a picture.

Of course, I'm not very famous. But I am a bit famous. People recognise me, and when they recognise me, they – by and large – feel comfortable about approaching me. I don't manage my image or pretend on television to be someone that I am not. I am what I am. Always. And I like to think people respond to this. I hope this is what they respond to. That they appreciate the fact that I am genuine. Opinionated – yes; occasionally gobby – yes; irritating – of course. But never less than myself.

The television work I have done tends to reinforce this. The advert for Paddy Power, for example, in which I was submerged in a bath, suddenly appearing from beneath the water, dressed in full Wednesday kit, to the startled punter who was sharing the water. I suppose it showed that I didn't much mind taking the piss out of myself. There certainly wasn't much money in it. Still, having said that, Mr. Paddy and Mr. Power did, later, invite me over to Ireland because they wanted to have lunch with me. I said I couldn't go because I had to pick up my daughter from school, so they sent a private plane, flew me over, gave me a great lunch at the Burlington Hotel, and then flew me back so I could do the school run in time. Mad.

Anyway, you have to remember that people's perceptions of you, their willingness to approach you or talk to you, depends largely on the opinions they might form after watching you on television. The other non-footballing television 'appearance' I made was on Channel 4's *Come Dine With Me – Footballers Special*.

When my agent first asked me whether I was interested, I more or less told him to fuck off; I'd been made to feel uncomfortable by the BBC, I couldn't cook (I mean, I *really* couldn't cook … not a thing), and I didn't know who was going to be on the programme. It was Lucy who persuaded me to give it a go. She liked the programme and thought it would be fun. Plus, it might raise my profile, something I was crap at doing. Also, if it turned out to be a relatively painless way to make a few bob and could lead to other things – why not?

The other three participants were all good blokes, too, which was fortunate. I'm not good at hiding my feelings about people and didn't want to come across as a cunt. John Fashanu, Frank Worthington, and Neil 'Razor' Ruddock. I knew Razor not only from playing against him but also from our time together with the England U21 team. We even roomed together. He was not only very competitive but also extremely funny. Worthington I knew by reputation and he had become something of a cult figure in the north, where he now lived. I had played against Fashanu and knew three things about him. First, he was intelligent. Second, I thought I liked him. Third, and not unrelated to the second point, he was dangerous. By that, I mean he could suddenly switch from charm to violence, and the switch could be flicked at any time. He had a certain presence about him on the football field, an aura, something that shouted loud and clear: 'Beware, handle with care'. He and Mick Harford were the only two footballers I played against who demanded that you be nice to them. I never wound Fashanu up and I always made a point to ask him, politely, how he was doing. Plus he was a martial arts expert and, I gather, could handle knives. Much as I liked him, you didn't fuck with Fash.

One other thing: I wanted to win. I want to win every competition I enter, even one that involves cooking and hospitality. Originally, and taking into account my chronic inability to cook, I considered ordering food in. Lucy told me not to be daft; I would come across as an idiot.

So I went to see Chris Kent, a Michelin-star chef, who was also a friend. He put together a menu that included sea bass and a couple of other dishes (including dessert) whose names I couldn't even pronounce. I think they were French. I thought, if I can't even say them, how am I going to cook them?

'Who the fuck's going to cook that?' I said to Chris when he presented his menu to me.

'You are,' he replied. 'It's actually simple to do.'

Then he showed me how to prepare the food, how to cook it, and finally how to present it on the plate.

It looked impossible. I watched what he did, made notes, and had a go.

It was awful. A car crash of food.

I had another go. This looked more like it. Chris threw it away.

'That's not what I asked you to do,' he growled.

I tried again. Chris threw it away again.

Eventually, I produced something that passed Chris' scrutiny. He tasted it.

'Bloody awful, Carlton,' he announced. 'Do it again.'

So I did it again. And again. And again. Every night in the week building up to the programme, Lucy arrived home to find me hunched over the cooker or chopping vegetables.

'What are we having?' she asked on the first evening.

'Sea bass.'

'Anything else?'

'Yes.'

'Well?'

Well what?'

'Well, what else?'

'Don't ask.'

'I am asking.'

'I can't say.'

'Is it a secret?'

'No. It's not a secret. I really can't say. It's French.'

By the end of the week, I had little idea of how good my cooking had become. I had made the sea bass and whatever it was we had with it every night for eight days. Lucy was sick of the sight of sea bass. Half way through the week, she asked if we could eat something else. Or, better, just go out for a meal.

'I've had it with the sea bass, Carlton. I don't think I can eat it again.'

'Only three more days,' I said.

'What are the others doing?'

'I don't know. But I bet they're not doing sea bass.'

'Maybe I'll join you, then. Just to eat something else.'

'Not long now. I think I'm getting it right.'

'I hope so. It's driving me mad.'

'No point in being in the programme if you don't want to win.'

'It's a cookery show. Not the World Cup.'

'Doesn't matter. Winning is still winning.'

'Jesus, Carlton.'

The thing is, I had built an entire career on winning and just being in competition with other people, no matter what the nature of the competition, brought out the combative instinct in me. I wanted to win. And, perhaps shamefully, I wanted to win badly.

The filming was done very quickly. On Thursday and Friday we were in London (for Fash and Razor), then on Monday and Tuesday we headed up north (for Frank and me).

I enjoyed doing the programmes very much. They were also great fun. Razor opened the front door to his home dressed only in an apron, his vast and very visible buttocks wobbling like a couple of mislaid camel humps. 'He's ballooned in size,' observed Fashanu, who is very conscious of the way he looks. 'I wasn't sure if it was Razor Ruddock coming to meet me or a horse.' As I said before, you don't answer back to men like Fash, no matter how insulting he is.

Off camera, and on two separate occasions, Frank (who was in the early stages of Alzheimer's) asked Fashanu about his brother. 'How's Justin these days?' was the way Frank phrased it. It wasn't a good question to ask. Justin had been dead for 12 years. He committed suicide in 1998, following his arrest in America for sexual assault on a seventeen-year old boy. The note he left said that he didn't feel he would get a fair trial because of his homosexuality and that he didn't want to cause embarrassment to his family and friends. Two years later, Fash said he wasn't sure if his brother really was gay and that he might merely have been seeking attention. Whatever the truth of it, Frank asking about Justin, twice, was not helpful. The second time, coincidentally, Fash happened to be in the kitchen. He was playing around with some knives, showing his dexterity in handling them, and there was a look in his eye. He was spinning them in hands, twisting and manipulating them like a knife-thrower in a circus. Razor ushered Frank away, saying, 'Let's go and have a have a drink, Frank, and let Fash get on with the cooking.'

When we went to Huddersfield for Frank's dinner, no one could find him. The television crew, who had arrived early to set up, hadn't seen him all day. And when we started to arrive, there was still no Frank. Eventually, he was tracked down to a local pub. He'd forgotten about the programme and gone boozing. We joined him and I had ten pints before the filming even started.

The four nights were hard work but great fun. I don't remember much about the food except that it was pretty basic – shepherd's pie comes to mind, for example – and I felt my sea bass, which I had more or less perfected by this time, and so long as I didn't fuck it up on the night, would win the day. The evening at my place was to be the last one, but before that there was an Elvis-themed dinner (Frank idolised the King and at one point in his career even had an Elvis hairdo). Wanting to win this, too, if dressing up as

Elvis can be called a competition, I made sure I had all the gear, including a massive rubberised Elvis wig.

I spent all day preparing the food, chopping up the vegetables with military precision and even chucking away the first lot I did because the carrots weren't the right shape. The television crew arrived early to find me hard at it in the kitchen, though I hardly noticed them as I was in the zone. All the practice with Chris Kent had turned me into a kind of well-grooved chef machine: I was completely focused, as if my whole life depended on the light grilling of a small fish. But that's the way I was. That's the way I am.

When Lucy arrived home from work I was still at it.

'Bloody hell, Carlton. You've been at that all day.'

'Quiet, Lucy. I'm concentrating.'

'What? Concentrating on food?'

'I'm doing the dessert. So fuck off,' I said, without even looking up.

We then had a loud, full-on row, yelling at each other and turning the air blue with language. She stomped upstairs, changed her clothes, and then flounced out of the house. I had to apologise to the television crew, who were very embarrassed by it all, give them a drink, and then get back to what I really wanted to do, i.e. be in the kitchen.

The evening went well and when Lucy returned, we were all still drinking and making a lot of noise. She turfed us out at about 2 a.m. and we went to Chris's restaurant, where we continued to booze until 7.

The show received good reviews and people said they'd seen a different side to me. What they actually meant was that they'd seen me cook rather than play football. But in point of fact, and in reality, it wasn't such a different side. The same Carlton Palmer – wants to do something well, gives it his complete attention, trains hard, doesn't give a stuff how he is perceived.

I say all this because people's perception of me these days is mediated by what they see on television. I don't do much but what I do manages, just, to keep me in the public eye. Although I'm not necessarily a familiar figure, I am at least *familiar*. People feel they know me. And programmes like *Come Dine With Me*, while they might not lead to other things (as they did, by the way, for a couple of the others), remind people who I am. Perhaps in some unconscious way I still need the recognition? But as I'm no good at pretending to be something I'm not, they kind of feel comfortable with me. Always, I am what I am. There is very little side to me, no guile, no strategy, no deviousness. Which is why people in The Camel felt they could approach me and chat without feeling uncomfortable or intimidated.

Afterwards, I rolled home at about 2 or 3 in the morning (Wednesday had lost to a good Hull side; Steve Bruce is a decent man, so fair play to him), though only after being helped into the lift and taken to my front door by the concierge, waking up Lucy, being banished to the spare room, and spending much of the night on the toilet.

In the morning, Lucy had an appointment to see the doctor about a skin complaint, which she blames on being in China. She likes being in Shanghai but I don't think she likes it as much as I do. Sometimes I feel as if she's looking for an excuse to get back to Sheffield.

'It's the water and the air,' she said.

'What's the water and the air?' I replied.

'My skin.'

'There's nothing wrong with your skin.'

'There is something wrong with my skin. It's dry. And

blotchy.'

'Not really. Besides, even if it was dry and blotchy – which it isn't – how do you know it's the water and the air that causes it?'

'Come on, Carlton. Don't be thick. The pollution.'

'It was worse in London yesterday.'

'I don't believe you.'

'You can check if you like. More polluted in London than Shanghai.'

'You're talking bollocks.'

'And what about your hair?'

'It's getting thin. The water's no good for it here.'

'My hair's fine.'

'You haven't got any hair. You shave it all off.'

'I've got plenty of hair. I just choose not to let it grow.'

'Well, if you did let it grow, the Chinese water would get to it.'

'No it wouldn't.'

'Yes it would.'

'One of the chemistry teachers told me that the water here is fine. She also said that it's better than the water in England. She reckons English men go bald because of English water.'

'Is that the Chinese chemistry teacher?'

'Might be.'

'Well, then.'

'There's nothing wrong with the water.'

'Why do you like living here so much? You don't normally like big cities. And Shanghai is bigger than almost any other city on the planet.'

She has a point. And asks a good question. I don't like living in big cities. Sheffield is ideal for me. London is too big.

Maybe Shanghai is so big that size has ceased to be an issue. All I know is that I feel very comfortable here. The Chinese don't give two fucks what anyone thinks. I like that. You can wear what you like and do what you like. Things that would draw stares, snobbishness and ridicule in England are accepted here without a second thought. If you want to wear purple trainers with brown polka dot trousers and a silver T-shirt, that's fine. Go ahead. Although the English media make a big thing about Chinese compliance, nobody here feels they have to conform in the routines of their daily lives. Anything goes. You see extraordinary things walking round Shanghai – mad, strange things that make me laugh. Bicycles with fifty chairs stuck to them, people walking backwards, OAPs dancing unselfconsciously in the park, old women doing the splits. They also work hard and from my experience are pretty straight when they deal with you. Plus our standard of living is high. We've been on holidays to the Maldives, Bali, the Philippines, and Malaysia. Lucy has become a diving instructor. There are great restaurants and there's plenty to do. Plus, football is like a drug. When you stop playing the game it's very difficult. You still need it in some way. You need *something*. You need something else. Ex-players have various ways of dealing with the disappearance of football from their daily routine. Maybe one of the reasons I don't mind being on television is because I can remind people that I, Carlton Palmer, am still here. It's part of the jigsaw. For the moment, and for the foreseeable future, Shanghai is what I need.

'You said that about Dubai,' Lucy says, after we've rehearsed the usual arguments about staying or not staying in China.

'Maybe,' I said, 'but Shanghai feels different.'

She's more of a home-bird than me. I'm also less enamoured with England than I used to be. It's not the place it was. And I feel I'm able to do more with my life living abroad than I would at home. The job's good. I enjoy the feeling that I am working for a living, that I am earning a crust, that I have a proper identity. Even perhaps with the academy that I am building something here. Life is good.

I am Carlton Palmer, ex-England footballer, and I don't need to smoke marijuana.

18

The Kindness of Women

'The course of true love never did run smooth.'
William Shakespeare – *A Midsummer Night's Dream*

I remember playing against Stan Collymore when he was at Liverpool and enjoying an especially rich vein of form. He was quick, skilful and strong, with a bit of the devil about him. In other words, a real handful. Those were the days when referees allowed you one free hit before they reached for a yellow card. It's not like that now – go anywhere near someone, let alone tackle them, and it's an automatic booking. Anyway, I knew that I had to make my first proper tackle on Collymore worthwhile and effective. Use my free hit in a telling and purposeful way. So I watched and waited for seventeen minutes, biding my time. Then, he received the ball square on to me and in a bit of space. I was about a metre or so away. Instinctively, he began to turn, to put his body between me and the ball. I made a decision to go in hard and to take the ball by going through his supporting leg, calculating that if I did it quickly and cleanly enough, and even if I was a little late, the referee would have no choice but to see it as a clumsy but legitimate tackle. I would probably get away with it altogether. There was a chance I would concede a free kick. A yellow card would be highly unlikely, no matter what kind of contact I made. Collymore saw me beginning to slide in and began to move in the opposite direction, taking the ball with him but in the process further exposing his supporting leg. I was fully committed and knew exactly what I was doing – focused on the ball and wilfully oblivious to anything between it and my boot … including Collymore's leg. It all happened in a split second. Boot, leg, ball. My long leg meant I was able to get to the ball more quickly than he'd anticipated. As he tried to lift his leg out of harm's way, I caught it square on, shifting it unceremoniously to one side, and raked the ball towards me. As I brought my own leg back, I caught Collymore's trailing foot for the second time. Although I had the ball, I knew I'd hurt him. That was, after all, the intention. I mean, not to injure him, but to cause him pain, to let him know I was *there*, to make him think twice every time he received the ball, to make him think about me bearing down on him.

Actually, the tackle caused more damage than I'd intended. Collymore limped off a few minutes later. Did I care? Of course not. Not a jot. No lasting damage to him and a dangerous player had been removed from the game. I had simply done my job as a professional footballer. And as a professional footballer, I embraced – consciously and completely embraced – many characteristics that people who don't play elite sport don't understand. Or can't appreciate. That is, the attributes of dogged resolve, niggling efficiency, and a lack of 'style' for style's sake. Nothing else matters to the truly professional sportsman. But in England, the legacy of amateurism lives on. Fans still expect the qualities of 'sportsmanship' and 'grace' to persist. It's a romantic view of the game that is at odds with the contemporary game. If fans really tolerated the full implications of professional football, then every game would be played in an openly cynical spirit. A so-called 'professional foul' would be applauded, merely because it could be shown to have prevented the other side gaining an advantage. A defender sent off for deliberately hurting an opposing player would be cheered all the way to the dressing room. (I would have been saluted as the cause of Collymore leaving the field.)

These things do happen, of course, but by and large football hasn't yet been reduced to these depths. And I am glad. Despite having myself been an absolutely professional footballer – whose strengths were resolve, efficiency, and a lack of style – I like the idea of elegance and flair on the football field. It stirs something in me even if, on occasions, what it stirs is the desire to stamp it out.

I've changed. Football has changed me. Of course football has changed me. All I've known since the age of fifteen is football. Sometimes I think it's all I've ever known. And in some ways, just as the changes in football over the past twenty or thirty years reflect the changes in English life, so they reflect the changes in me, too.

What, I sometimes wonder, has happened to the Carlton Palmer who stood on the terraces at the Hawthorns, watching Albion, and dreaming in an uncomplicated way of becoming a footballer? You could get a season ticket and watch your heroes for about twenty quid. On Saturday mornings, you'd quite often bump into the players doing a bit of shopping in Sandwell or West Bromwich. Football was part of life but also distinct from it. Footballers were footballers while they played football. Afterwards, they could become something else. These days, once a footballer, always a footballer – even when you've stopped playing. Playing the game leaves an indelible mark. The money, the intensity, the sense of being different from other people, the exaggerated feeling of being a symbol of Englishness ... of past glories and post-Imperial decline, of being a minor celebrity, of being representative of a distinctive English style of play (muscular, honest, uncomplicated), of a tolerance of black players and a kind of sporting multiculturalism.

I can't deny that I felt these last two quite keenly.

It gets to you. It gets inside you. At any rate, it got to me. Now I think in football.

A few weeks ago, Lucy and I had an argument. It was over something trivial and silly, and she asked why I had acted in a particular way.

'What do you mean?' I said.

'Why did you behave like that?'

'Like what?'

'Like you did.'

'I don't know. I just did.'

'Can you explain it?'

'Sometimes people act in ways they can't explain.'

'Don't be an idiot. Everything has a reason.'

'Not everything. This doesn't.'

'Really?!'

'Think of it like this, Lucy. I remember once that Wednesday were playing Arsenal. They were on a bad run and had injuries. A young kid was called in to play centre forward for them. Kevin Campbell. We were playing well, put out our strongest team, and were confident we'd turn them over. I think we were 3-0 down at half time. Maybe four down. Campbell scored twice. When we got in at half time, we were expecting a right bollocking. But the manager didn't shout at us. He didn't rant. He just said, "There's no rhyme or reason for this. It's just one of those things. So let's forget it and put it behind us. It's inexplicable." And that's what this is, Lucy. Don't you see? It's the same thing. It's unaccountable.'

'For fuck's sake, Carlton.'

'What?'

'That's football. This is *life*.'

She's right, of course.

But I have a habit of seeing everything, life included, as football. As something that can be approached, resolved and dealt with like a game of football. It's a drug. Rules, regularity, pragmatism, hard work, reward, focus and winning. Always winning. There's even a streak of cynicism in me, a world-weariness that knows how I must sometimes behave in order to get the job done. A streak of cynicism that absolutely understands what Roy Keane recently said about needing to foul a player if it was the only way of stopping him. A streak of cynicism that is constantly at odds with the naïve, romantic idealist who a long time ago stood on the terraces at Albion and dreamed of becoming a footballer. Whose dream extended not much further than longing for a life in which he made ends meet by kicking a ball around and being seen as a good man, a good family man, with a wife and family, whose parents were proud of him. Somewhere inside me that man still exists. He fights to get out, to make himself heard. But sometimes it's a fucking hard slog.

Wounds have been inflicted. Leading an existence in which I'm used to setting and being set targets, of seeing everything in black and white, of seeing life as a series of binary opposites, of understanding it merely as a journey of achievement and reward, of success and failure, of constantly having to be strong and thick-skinned while at the same time nursing hurts and sensitivities … these things leave scars.

I sometimes ask myself how I manage to function *at all* as a human being in the world beyond football.

I think the answer is the women in my life.

I have two sisters (Julie and Sharon), two daughters (and a son), plus a step-daughter. But I suppose my appreciation of women comes from my mother, whose values and character have made such a strong impression on me and who constantly reminds me of the person I ought to be.

Although her name is Linda, dad always calls her 'Cherry'. They met in Jamaica and have been together for over fifty years. There is a goodness and solidity about her that shames me and prompts any self-awareness I might have. She still sends stuff back to Jamaica, to people she barely knows, virtual strangers, simply because they are somehow connected to relatives who might have mentioned them. She knows her place (in that sense, her relationship with dad is very traditional), though she has always kept him in line, exerting influence in a roundabout, indirect way. She operates in a much more subtle way than the male Palmers, avoiding confrontation, keeping her counsel, and being patient. She was a little wary of Lucy when they first met, perhaps worried that I would not be well looked after. 'Are you good at playing mum?' she asked Lucy at a BBQ in the garden.

Being a mother, of course, is not merely about pampering. Whenever I Skype my mum and dad, she often finds fault – for example about my teeth being too yellow or me being overweight. Although I know she is just playing the concerned mother and making it clear that she is still the boss, I always take immediate action to put things right. She has expectations of me and I am still very vulnerable to her judgement. 'Like a little boy,' Lucy often teases.

The Skype conversations tend to start off with me talking to my dad. They are usually about politics or something that we've both seen on the news. There's very little talk about family or feelings. Mum is in the background, often doing something else, pottering but hovering and somehow very present. When she appears on the screen, she frequently and immediately says something personal and discerning.

'You look ill, Carlton. Have you been eating properly?'

'What have you done with your hair, Carlton? It doesn't look right.'

'Your skin looks tired, Carlton. Have you been getting enough rest?'

Because dad was usually working, it was always mum who came to watch me play football, even though she didn't know much about the game.

Afterwards, she would say things like, 'Carlton, you mustn't spit so much,' or 'Carlton, you must try to control your temper. Do you have to push the other players?' Never anything about the game itself. Always about things like my spitting or not tucking my shirt in or, on one occasion, telling me off for picking my nose in a game against Everton.

Mum and dad are Christians and we used to go to church every Sunday. Looking back, I think this was more to do with being part of a community than any belief in a divinity, an Almighty Being, overseeing our lives, though the sense of godliness has stayed with me. At my first England get-together, I couldn't stop myself saying grace when the squad was eating a communal meal. The other players were astonished and I never did it again. Even so, I occasionally have a chat with God and can't dismiss the possibility that He exists. Lucy, incidentally, is a Catholic.

What I've got from mum and dad is a determination to do things properly. Before he drove buses, dad was in the army, and he bequeathed me the regimentation from that life. Mum and dad's religious beliefs bestowed on me a belief in rules and rituals. Some of these things are natural allies of the elite sportsman, though the world of professional football mashes them up in peculiar ways. I do most things to excess – obsessively, compulsively, almost neurotically, traits which are also, in point of fact, the characteristics of a successful sportsman and in particular of a footballer. What I've got specifically from mum is a sense of the importance of manners, kindness and thoughtfulness. Which isn't to say that I am at all times well-mannered, kind and thoughtful. When I fail in these areas, it is her voice I hear in my head.

Wives and girlfriends don't like to hear they resemble mothers, though it is certainly true that, like my mum, Lucy is kind and instinctively puts herself out to help others. Maybe at some level I do see my mum in Lucy, or rather recognition of the values she embodies. I am a compulsive and excessive man, a difficult man, whose behaviour can be extreme and who is probably – let's face it – addicted to alcohol. When Lucy and I argue, the disagreements are usually alcohol-related. Booze is my habit and occasionally my problem. Its intoxicating effect is in part a renewal of the professional highs I experienced as well as a reminder and a memento of those heady days. It's not an uncommon phenomenon amongst ex-footballers. During those moments when I behave in unreasonable, pathological and dangerous ways, Lucy is the one who keeps me reasonably calm and more or less in line. She is more considered and philosophical than me. I respect her even when I think she's wrong. And because I'm Carlton Palmer, I will probably always think she is wrong. I am strong and wilful and stubborn and impetuous. There are no grey areas in my life. I am always right and I can't say 'sorry'. I am insecure and needy and affectionate and I need someone to say she loves me, like my mum always did. But it can't be anyone and it has to mean something. I ask a lot of Lucy. How can someone who knows me like she does say she loves me and sincerely *mean it* and, more to the point, persuade me that she means it? Taking me on is a difficult job. Maybe an impossible one. Certainly a time-consuming and frustrating one. Lucy it was who ripped off my special lucky underpants, which I'd refused to discard because I associated them with winning. Lucy it is who picks up the pieces whenever I fall out with my kids. Lucy it was who put me back together after I'd run away to Dubai to escape Jenny's influence, though in the process pushing away my children. There are two sides to me and Lucy fixes them together. When my kids say that I use money to control them and I counter by explaining that I'm just trying to give them lives free from hardship, it's Lucy who sees both sides of the argument and somehow reconciles them. (I once had a competition with David Hirst to see which of us could spend the most money in the shortest amount of time. I lost. He bought a car.) Lucy it is who reins me in, grounds me, and makes me see myself for the twat I can sometimes be. Formed by my parents and my profession and, yes, of my own character, I have plunged into the roar of time and the whirl of accident. Pain and pleasure, success and failure, have shifted as they will. And it is only through the kindness of women that I have been able to continue.

And now the kindness of these women, and especially the kindness and understanding of Lucy, is being stretched to the limit.

A little over two years ago, I was playing squash with Sean, the Australian tennis coach in Shanghai. He was beating me and, of course, I was determined not to be beaten, so perhaps I pushed myself too hard. Whatever, my heart started racing, galloping wildly out of control. I managed to slow it down and although there was clearly something wrong and although Lucy told me to get it checked, I didn't take myself to hospital. Typical man. Predictable Carlton.

The same thing happened a few times after that. Always, I managed to control my heart rate. I convinced myself that sheer will power would allow me to contain whatever was wrong and, furthermore, that if will power could contain the problem, then the problem couldn't have been very significant.

Then, during a friendly game of football, I started to feel unwell. Similar symptoms as before. My heart racing, light-headedness and sweating. I excused myself from the match and went straight to the bathroom, believing I could, as usual, fix the problem myself. I splashed myself with cold water. I took an aspirin. I willed my heart to slow down. It had worked before and it would work this time.

Except it didn't.

My heart continued to speed up. It was getting quicker and quicker. I tried to pull myself together and to bully my heart, ordering it to slow down. This time, it paid no attention to me. I stumbled into the school medical centre. The nurse took my blood pressure, said there was a problem with my heart – *I knew there was a problem with my heart* – and that I would have to go to hospital. Immediately. An ambulance arrived and I was given an injection and medication to bring my heart rate down.

At the hospital, I was given tests and a cardioversion, which is when two hand-held 'paddles' are placed on your chest, converting an abnormally fast heart rate to a normal rhythm through electric shocks. I stayed in overnight and during the next few days went through more tests. Under observation on a treadmill, I pushed my heart rate up to 155/160 (it is normally 45/50). No problem. I had an MRI scan. No problem. I swallowed dye to check for blocked arteries. No problem.

Therefore, I concluded, there was no problem.

I had a good reason for persuading myself. I had been invited to play football for England's Veterans against Germany's Veterans in Singapore. The game was just over a month away.

I asked the heart specialist whether I should play, though in my mind I had already made the decision.

No problem.

'Better that you don't play, Carlton,' he said.

'But all the tests said there was no problem,' I replied.

'There's no apparent medical reason why you shouldn't play … but it's best not to.'

'So there's no real problem?'

'It's best not to play.'

'I'll be careful.'

'As I said, my advice would be not to play.'

Five weeks later, I was in Singapore, warming up before the game, and not feeling great. The game against the Germans was being played in an indoor arena, so I put my discomfort down to the intense heat and humidity. About twenty into the game itself I was desperate for water, again blaming the clammy airlessness of the venue. I was also making uncharacteristic and basic mistakes, attributing it to the fact that I hadn't played for a while.

'Are you ok?' Paul Parker asked me.

'I'm fine,' I replied.

'You look like shit, Carlton,' he persisted.

'I'll be fine,' I said, though I agreed to come off the pitch for a few minutes. The team doctor, who'd obviously seen what was happening, asked me to sit down for a few minutes.

At that point, I felt my heart accelerating again, going quickly through the gears, then suddenly losing any semblance of control. The thing inside my chest felt like it was trying to escape, writhing disobediently, almost as if it was no longer part of me. Instantly, sweat began to pour from my body. Apparently, I changed colour, becoming grey and then a kind of dirty beige. At the same time, I felt faint. Everything inside me seemed to stop, except for my heart, which felt as if it would burst apart. Before I knew what was happening, I was being led down the tunnel to the dressing room. I can remember my shirt being ripped off and being bundled into an ambulance and taken to hospital. I can't recall much of the journey except that I called Lucy, babbling on, convinced I was going to die, telling her I loved her. My hands and feet went numb and I fumbled the phone. Believing these were my last minutes, the whole world contracted. My sole point of focus was now the phone. If I could make the call, then I would die a contented man. In the space of five minutes I had gone from feeling ill, passing through fear for my life, to accepting that my existence would surely end. At the hospital, I was shovelled onto a trolley. My heart rate was at 220. One nurse shouted, 'He's going to go into cardiac ...!' Someone else bellowed, 'Quickly! Quickly!' And all I could think about was my long arms and legs, hanging awkwardly off the side of the gurney, supposing it was a bloody stupid way to die ...

That was all I could remember because I was then given an injection that knocked me unconscious. Two 'paddles' were attached to my chest and a surge of electricity jolted through me. It didn't work so they increased the dose and repeated the procedure. This time, my heart started and jerked back into some kind of rhythm.

Of course, I wasn't aware of any of this. I woke up in a hospital bed, tubes snaking their ways into and out of my body. The doctor – Dr. Meng: how I love that man – said I was very lucky and that they'd had to use a high voltage to get my heart going. The bruises on my chest were livid, two angry circles of violence. Three months later, you can still see them.

When Dr. Meng explained the cause of the problem, it sounded both banal and obvious. I was born with a part of my heart branching off. This is known as a pulmonary CTV, where the right superior pulmonary vein has an independent branch. Blood was simply not getting through to my heart.

I thought of all the medicals I'd had as a professional footballer. Of all the medicals I'd had since I'd stopped playing. And I considered the regular and rigorous fitness regimes I'd subjected myself to. On the one hand, it all seemed so unfair and ill-fated. How could my body, which was thrashed into good shape on a daily basis, be vulnerable to something like this? On the other hand, I was lucky. Lucky it happened in Singapore, where the medical treatment is excellent. Lucky it happened at a football tournament, where top quality help was immediately available. And lucky that I was so fit, something that kept me alive between collapsing and getting to hospital.

A few weeks later, I had surgery in Shanghai – an AFib and flutter ablation – the doctors going in through my groin in an attempt to widen my arteries. The flutter has been cured but the AFib could reoccur.

Lucy told me that my behaviour before the operation reminded her of the way I used to prepare for games, talking to myself, telling myself I could beat it. 'Come on. Let's go. It's showtime! Nothing's going to beat us. Come on!'

And that's part of the problem. Since I was a teenager, I have been used to overcoming obstacles through willpower and effort. If there was a difficulty, I would size it up, work out a way to confront it, and then get the better of it. But my heart was and still is out of my control. It squats inside me, an alien thing, a potential enemy, and beyond my jurisdiction. I have to love my heart now and look after it, but at the same time I hate it. I hate its unruliness and delinquency. I hate the fact that even though it's inside me and is mine, I no longer have absolute authority over it. It's unreliable and troublesome and disobedient.

Despite the success of the operation, the experience has changed me. There's no doubt about that. My imperfection is loathsome to me. I have always hated the idea of being a burden to anyone and although I am trying hard not to be one, I suspect I am. I seek reassurance, even about the times I am supposed to be taking my tablets. I hear myself apologising to Lucy for the demands I make on her. I hate taking medication as I believe it's a sign of weakness. In the past, even if I had a headache, I would refuse painkillers, preferring to grit my teeth and get through it unaided. But now my fallibility is evident on a daily basis. You can't change genetics. And my dad has had three heart attacks.

To counteract this, I have decided not to change my lifestyle. I will continue to train and train hard. If I get the chance to play football, I will. And I'll still drink. Of course I'll drink. Training and playing and drinking. That's my life. The future will be the same as my past, even if this means there is a possibility the future will not be quite as extended as it once might have been.

A few months ago, at Christmas, I drank too much. Lucy was furious and even told my mum about it. I listened to what she was saying but I need the drink. I need the buzz. This is what football has given me and I'll be buggered if I'm going to give it up. I am Carlton Palmer. I am Carlton Palmer and more than ever I am testing the kindliness and understanding of Lucy, who tells me that I have turned, once more, into a little boy. More than ever I need her, I need it, her kindness, the kindness of women.

About the Authors

Carlton Palmer began his football career as a YTS player at his local club West Bromwich Albion while still a teenager, and quickly made a name for himself as a combative midfielder. He established a rapport with The Baggies' manager Ron Atkinson who persuaded Carlton to follow him when he took the reins at Sheffield Wednesday.

Carlton's determined, battling style endeared him to the Hillsborough faithful, and to then England manager Graham Taylor who selected him to represent his country on eighteen occasions.

Making over two hundred appearances for Wednesday, Carlton was transferred to Leeds United in 1994 for a fee of £2.6 million. Three years later he moved to Southampton for two seasons before joining Nottingham Forest and then Coventry City.

Since retiring from playing, Carlton has worked as a football coach and TV pundit. He is now based in China where he is the academy director at Wellington College International in Shanghai.

Steven Jacobi has published several novels and books of non-fiction. He collaborated with the actor Sir Ian Holm in the writing of his autobiography. In addition, he has written drama and documentaries for the BBC, and journalism for a number of newspapers and magazines.

With an academic background and a PhD in English Literature, Steven has taught across the world and organised many literary festivals, whose participants have included Melvyn Bragg, John le Carre, Sir Trevor McDonald and many others.

Steven was a Royal Literary Fellow at Warwick University and is currently working and writing in Shanghai. He supports Birmingham City.